Bhaktisūtras of Nārada

Bhaktisūtras of Nārada

translated by

Nandalal Sinha

Munshiram Manoharlal
Publishers Pvt. Ltd.

Dedicated to the
Sacred Memory of
Rai Bahadur Srisachandra Vasu Vidyarnava

ISBN 81-215-0827-4
Second revised edition 1998
First published 1918

Typeset, printed and published by
Munshiram Manoharlal Publishers Pvt. Ltd.,
Post Box 5715, 54 Rani Jhansi Road, New Delhi 110 055.

Contents

Introduction

There is a tradition as to the origin and authorship of this short treatise (vide *Śrīmadbhāgavatam*, chaps. 1, 4 and 5). Maharṣi Vedavyāsa was staying in his hermitage of Badarikāśrama. One day the celestial hermit Nārada turned up there in the course of his usual wanton rambles. The great Vyāsa welcomed him with due rites, and, on his taking seat, asked: "Prophet of Gods! the soul of man seeks to get free from the hold of pleasure and pain, and craves for deliverance from the bondage of the world. But the path of Action (*karma*) does not lead directly to the goal. Knowledge (*jñāna*) of course, does; nevertheless, without the leaven of Devotion, it can achieve very little in substance. Devotion (*bhakti*) is the only way of attaining salvation; all the others have importance only insofar as they are auxiliary to it. Therefore I humbly ask you to explain to me the doctrine of Devotion." The divine Nārada at once surveyed the mind of Vyāsa, and replied: "Great sage! you have come down on earth for the redemption of mankind. Your present enquiry has been prompted by that desire alone. By your disciple Jaimini, you have already, in the Pūrvamīmāṃsā, discoursed upon the problem of Action, and have yourself completed the enquiry into the problem of Knowledge in the Uttaramīmāṃsā. And now you have taken up the problem of Devotion. I am going to explain it. But its full explanation will be given by you in your *Śrīmadbhāgavatam* which will be of the nature of a commentary upon your *Brahmsūtras*. My *sūtras* will be read as such in explanation of your very short description of Devotion given in the Uttaramīmāṃsā."

So saying, Nārada delivered a discourse on Devotion in 84 aphorisms the collection of which forms this short treatise, known as *Nārada Bhaktisūtram* (*Bhaktisūtras of Nārada*).

The doctrine of Devotion, however, is as old as the Vedas where it has been revealed as the Pañcarātra (Bhāgavata or Sātvata) Tantra. "The theory of the Bhāgavatas is that from Vāsudeva, who is the highest Brahman and the highest cause, there originates the individual soul called Saṅkarṣaṇa; from Saṅkarṣaṇa the internal organ called Pradyumna; and from Pradyumna the principle of egoity called Aniruddha." "What it teaches is that the highest Brahman, there called Vāsudeva, from kindness to those devoted to it, voluntarily abides in a fourfold form, so as to render itself accessible to its devotees. . . . That highest Brahman, called Vāsudeva, having for its body the complete aggregate of the six qualities, divides itself insofar as it is either the 'subtle' (*sūkṣma*), or 'division' (*vyūha*), or 'manifestation' (*vibhava*), and is attained in its fullness by the devotees who, according to their qualifications, do worship to it by means of work guided by knowledge. 'From the worship of the *vibhava*-aspect one attains to the *vyūha*, and from the worship of the *vyūha* one attains to the 'subtle' called Vāsudeva, i.e., the highest Brahman'—such is their doctrine. By the *vibhava* we have to understand the aggregate of beings such as Rāma, Kṛṣṇa, etc., in whom the highest Being becomes manifest; by the *vyūha* the fourfold arrangement or division of the highest Reality, as Vāsudeva, Saṅkarṣaṇa, Pradyumna, and Aniruddha; by the 'subtle' the highest Brahman itself; insofar as it has for its body the mere aggregate of the six qualities—as which it is called 'Vāsudeva'. "The Lord who is known from the Vedānta-texts, i.e., Vāsudeva, called there the highest Brahman—who is antagonistic to all evil, whose nature is of uniform excellence, who is an ocean, as it were, of unlimited exalted qualities, such as infinite intelligence, bliss, and so on, all whose purposes come true—perceiving that those devoted to him, according as they are differently placed in the four castes and the four stages of life, are intent on the different ends of life, viz. religious observances, wealth, pleasure, and final release, and recognising that the Vedas—which teach the truth about his own nature, his glorious manifestations, the means of rendering him propitious and the fruits of such endeavour—are difficult to fathom by all beings other than himself, whether gods or men, since those Vedas are divided into *Ṛk*, *Yajus*, *Sāman*, and *Atharvan*; and being animated by infinite pity, tenderness, and magnanimity; with a view to enable his devotees to grasp the true meaning of the Vedas, himself composed the *Pañcarātraśāstra*." (*Śrībhāṣya of Rāmānuja*, Thibaut's translation, *SBE*, vol. XLVIII, pp. 524-28.)

Nārada is a typical *bhakta* or devotee, and in his aphorisms he has breathed that enthusiasm of selfless devotion to God, which is all his own. Devotion is the highest sentiment that the human soul is capable of, and it is evident from the aphorisms that Nārada has dealt with the subject from the point of view of sentiment alone. The *Bhaktimīmāṃsā* of Śāṇḍilya, on the other hand, is, as its name implies, an enquiry into the philosophy of Devotion. Accordingly, the two treatises may be regarded as companion pieces, supplementing each other. We give below a summary of their teachings on some of the principal points embraced by the theme of Devotion.

The Doctrine of Devotion

I. *Its Philosophical Basis*

Jīva or the Embodied Self and Brahman or the Pure Self are two distinct realities. In the phenomenal world, as in the case of ordinary mortals, they stand apart from each other. Philosophy seeks to vindicate their existence and to ascertain the nature and attributes of each, while Religion seeks to find out the way for the *jīva*'s return to Brahman. Systems of thought and religion differ according as they take different views of the *jīva* and Brahman or of their relation to each other. Thus, the sage Kāśyapa thinks that the *jīva* is absolutely dissimilar to Brahman and that Brahman is higher than the *jīva* (Ś. 29*). According to the great Vyāsa, on the other hand, the notions of the *jīva* and Brahman are erroneous, and there is but one reality, viz., the Self in the from of pure consciousness (*Brahmasūtra*, IV.i.3; Ś. 30). Śāṇḍilya rejects both these extreme theories, and takes the middle course, thereby reconciling the two to a certain extent. His theory is that the *jīva* and Brahman are two distinct realities, but that, under the aspect of eternity, the *jīva* possesses the same nature as Brahman, which, however, does not belong to it, in a developed form, in the phenomenal world, in other words, that it is capable of attaining to, that is to say, returning to, *Brahma-bhāva* or the state of Brahman (Ś. 31). He gives reasons for his theory, and refers to authoritative texts (such as *Chāndogya Upaniṣad,* Adhyāya III, Khaṇḍa 14; *Taittirīya Saṃhitā,* VII.i.10.2; *Taittirīya Āraṇyaka,* III.11.4; *Taittirīya Upaniṣad*, III.1, the great saying, "Thou art That", *Gītā*, XV.7, et seq.), in support of it. It may be objected that the above theory involves a contradiction in thought, inasmuch as the ideas of being the Creator of the World, and the like, and of not being so are altogether different. To this Śāṇḍilya replies that there is no such contradiction here, in the same way as there is not any in the act of recognition, although there too the object present to the senses is different from the object recalled. Nor does it follow from this theory that Brahman also is subject to the limitations and sufferings peculiar to the *jīva*; for the very point of this theory is that limitations and sufferings are mere accidents and in no way appertain to the nature of the Self (Ś. 33). This does not, however, apply to the lordliness of Brahman characterised as the Creator, etc., for such lordliness belongs to its very essence (Ś. 34). Nowhere in the Śrutis the lordliness of Brahman has been denied, while it follows from the similarity of nature between the *jīva* and Brahman that limitations and sufferings are accidents in the life of the *jīva* (Ś. 35). An objector may argue

*Ś. refers to the aphorisms of Śāṇḍilya, while the figures give the numbers of the aphorisms.

that a time may come when, after the dissolution, one by one, of finite intellects (*buddhi*), all the *jīvas* will return into the state of Brahman, and when, in consequence, there will be no further occasion for the exercise of lordliness on the part of Brahman, so that lordliness as such cannot be a permanent and essential attribute of Brahman. To this Śāṇḍilya replies that no such time can possibly arrive, inasmuch as finite intellects, the limiting adjuncts of the *jīvas*, are infinite in number, and creation accordingly is an eternal process (Ś. 36). It may be urged, again, that Brahman being the material cause of the universe, it lacks the characteristic of immutability. But this is not the case. It is *Prakṛti, māyā* (Plato's Matter), which is really the material cause of the universe, while the causality of Brahman operates through the medium of *Prakṛti* (Ś. 37). Brahman is Pure Existence, *Prakṛti* is its Energy. Brahman does not become transformed under the influence of *Prakṛti*, as a magician is not transformed by his own magic. Hence the immutability of Brahman remains unimpaired. The words of the Śruti, which declare the world to be *situated* in Brahman, have been used figuratively, as a person seated on a chair within a room, may be said to be seated in the room as well as the chair (Ś. 38). Both Brahman and *Prakṛti* are indispensable, mutually dependent, causes of the universe (Ś. 39). That which knows is Brahman, that which is known is *Prakṛti*, and there is no middle term between them (Ś. 40). They are, therefore, eternally related. And because it is the Energy of Brahman, *Prakṛti* cannot be unreal (Ś. 41).

The *jīvas* emanate from Brahman, and participate in its existence. This emanation takes place by means of its will to be and its will to do, and is guided by its intelligence (Ś. 87 and 88). Having, thus, created beings of various grades, high and low, it composed the Vedas for their welfare (Ś. 89 and 90). And according to Bādarāyaṇa (vide *Vedāntasūtras*, I.i.2), it dispenses also the consequences of actions to the *jīvas* (Ś. 91). Dissolution consists in the relapse of these minor entities into the Supreme Being (Ś. 92).

Now, ultimately there is but one Self, and not many. Plurality of Selves is a phenomenon due to the association of *upādhis*, adjuncts or external limitations just as the phenomenon of plurality of suns may be produced by means of the application of a number of mirrors (Ś. 93). It cannot be argued that, because there exists a difference of status, that is, because some *jīvas* attain Release, while other remain in the state of bondage, therefore the *jīvas* must be absolutely dissimilar to one another, each possessing independent principles and spheres of intelligence and activity; for, in that case, there can be no relationship of the seer and the object seen between the Supreme Lord and the *jīvas*, and hence it would follow that omnipotence and omniscience do not belong to Him and that He is apprehensible by finite intelligences like any other object of cognition (Ś. 94). Besides, the circumstances which apparently differentiate the Self on the phenomenal plane, namely, individual cognitions, desires, feelings, volitions, etc., are not essential attributes of the Self, but have their origin elsewhere, and are merely reflected in it (Ś. 95). All the change, differentiation, that the Self undergoes, is its appearance on, and disappearance from, the field of phenomenal existence, where it comes into association with activity and its consequence (Ś. 100).

Mukti, Release, then means the return of the *saṃsārī jīva*, i.e., *jīva* as undergoing revolutions of births and deaths in ever-changing forms of existences, into the state of Brahman, the Pure Self, characterised as pure existence, pure consciousness, and pure bliss. The cause of *saṃsāra* or worldly existence is not want of knowledge. The argument that like the erroneous apprehension of a snake in a piece of rope, this world also has no foundation in reality, is not valid. For, in the first place, there is no adequate reason in favour of the supposition: on the other hand, were the world a creation of the imagination, the inference of God as the Cause of the world and fall to the ground. Nor has Bādarāyaṇa, in any of his aphorisms (the *Vedāntasūtras*), taught the unreality of the world; on the contrary, by showing the unreality of the dream-creation, he has established the reality of the creation of the waking state, and thereby disproved the theory that the world is the imagination of ignorance "We admit," says Rāmānuja in the *Śrībhāṣya*, "that release consists only in the cessation of Nescience, and that this cessation results from the knowledge of Brahman. But a distinction has here to be made regarding the nature of this knowledge which the Vedānta-texts aim at enjoining for the purpose of putting an end to Nescience. Is it merely the knowledge of the sense of sentences which originates from the sentences? or is it knowledge in the form of meditation (*upāsanā*) which has the knowledge just referred to as its antecedent?. . . . Hence we conclude that the knowledge which the Vedānta-texts aim at inculcating is a knowledge other than the mere knowledge of the sense of sentences, and denoted by *dhyāna*, *upāsanā* (i.e., meditation), and similar terms. . . .

" 'Meditation' means steady rememberance, i.e., a continuity of steady remembrance, uninterrupted like the flow of oil; in agreement with the scriptural passage which declares steady remembrance to be the means of release, on the attainment of remembrance all the ties are loosened. . . ." (*Ch. Up.*, VII.26.2)

"Such remembrance has been declared to be of the character of seeing," and this character of seeing consists in its possessing the character of immediate presentation (*pratyakṣatā*). With reference to remembrance, which thus acquires the character of immediate presentation and is the means of final release, scripture makes a further determination, viz., in the passage *Kaṭh Up.,* II.23. That Self cannot be gained by the study of the Veda (reflection), nor by thought (meditation), nor by much hearing. Whom the Self chooses, by him it may be gained; to him the Self 'reveals its being.' This text says at first that mere hearing, reflection, and meditation do not suffice to gain the Self, and then declares, "Whom the Self chooses, by him it may be gained." Now a 'chosen' one means a most beloved person; the relation being that he by whom that Self is held most dear is most dear to the Self. That the Lord (*Bhagavān*) himself endeavours that this most beloved person should gain the Self, he himself declares in the following words, "To those who are constantly devoted and worship with love I give that knowledge by which they reach me" (*Bh. G.*, X.10), and "To him who has knowledge I am dear above all things, and he is dear to me" (VII.17). Hence, he who possesses remembrance, marked by the character of immediate presentation (*sākṣātkāra*), and which itself is dear above all things, since the object remembered is such; he, we say, is chosen by the highest Self, and by him the highest Self is gained. Steady remembrance of this kind is designated by the word "Devotion (*bhakti*); for this term has the same meaning as *upāsanā* (meditation)." (Thibaut's translation, *SBE*, vol. XLVIII, pp. 11-16.)

The cause of *saṃsāra* accordingly is want to Devotion (Ś. 98). For, the fire of Devotion burns up the 'I' within the Self, i.e., the sense of separate personality, which is the direct cause or worldly existence, and the *jīva* attains to a state of perfect contentment, entire self-forgetfulness, and absolute identification of itself with Brahman; whereas want of Devotion implies the continuance of *ahaṃkāra,* egoity, the principle of individual separateness and agentship in the performance of acts for the realisation of desired ends, and consequently the state of feelings, volitions, attraction and repulsion pleasure and pain, and *dharma* and *adharma,* i.e., merits and demerits which necessarily lead to re-birth. That being so, the path of *mukti*, self-realization, return of the *jīva* into the state of Brahman, lies through single-hearted Devotion, inasmuch as Devotion frees the *jīva*, for ever, from the external limitation of the finite intellect which is a product of *Prakṛti* (Ś. 96). Freedom from the limitation of the finite intellect, again, has no necessary connection with freedom from the limitation of the physical organism. Success in the culture of Devotion may be attained even during the continue of life on earth, and in such cases the destined period of mortal existence has to be completed before final liberation can be enjoyed. The *jīva* which attains this state, is called *jīvan-mukta,* i.e., living, yet released. It is their *adṛṣṭam,* i.e., the potential after-effects of acts voluntarily performed by them, which stands in the way of their immediate release. It cannot be contended that similarly their other *adṛṣṭas* also, wherein they have reserved for them other experiences of worldly existence, must go on producing their effects, so that there can be no Release by means of Devotion; for, with the disappearance of *adṛṣṭam* determining length of life, and of the finite intellect, the very foundation of these other experiences are taken away from beneath them, inasmuch as experience of passing state is not an attribute of the Self, but is merely reflected in it from the finite intellect (Ś. 97).

An enquiry into the Doctrine of Devotion may be, therefore, profitably undertaken (Ś. 1, N.1*).

II. *Who are adhikārīs, i.e., entitled, to the Path of Devotion*

Jñāna, Knowledge of the truth about the Self and the Not-Self, and *karma*, religious performances, e.g., sacrifices, are not meant for all. For example, females and Śūdras are excluded from the study of the Vedas. But no such restriction exists in the case of Devotion. The Path of Devotion consists of a gradation of steps. The desire for *mukti*, the release from the coil of mortality, and the suffering attending it, is its starting point, and that which is called *parā bhakti,* i.e., Higher Devotion, is its goal; for, it is *parā bhakti* that immediately leads to *mukti* (Ś. 84). And subsidiary to *parā bhakti, ekānta-bhāva*, whole-hearted dovotion, there are various other forms of devotional states, eighty-one in number (vide *infra*, p.xix), and activities, which in their comprehensiveness reach from the highest to the lowest of human beings. Hence females, Śūdras, Caṇḍālas, and the like, as well as those who are better situated than they, are equally competent to follow the Path of Devotion: provided only they have awakened to the sense of their state as sinners and sufferers, and consequently have come to possess in all-absorbing desire for release from the painful revolutions of births and deaths. *Mumukṣutva,* desire for release, is the minimum qualification which entitles one to the Path of Devotion (Ś. 78-82; N. 33, 73).

III. *The Object of Devotion*

People worship minor deities, such as Indra and others, for the realization of particular objects of desire, e.g., learning, prosperity, relief

*N. refers to the aphorisms of Nārada, while the figures give the numbers of aphorisms.

from pain, etc., and these deities, being so worshipped, grant the prayers of their worshippers. Such worship is an act of Devotion. But the Devotion that is manifested in these cases, is of a lower kind. It is called *a-parā*, the lower, or *gauṇī,* the secondary, form of Devotion, as distinguished from what is called *parā*, the higher, or *mukhyā,* the primary, form of Devotion; for, not only is *mukti*, Release characterised as return into the state of Brahman, not attainable by *a-parā bhakti*, but it also fails to bring *abiding* peace to the soul, whereas, while *mukti* is the handmaid of *parā bhakti,* the latter also produces perfect peace of mind and constant enjoyment of pure bliss (N. 59-61). It has accordingly been taught that the Almighty *alone* should be worshipped, always with the whole heart, and with implicit faith (N. 80), and that, being invoked, He at once mainfests Himself, and fills His devotees with His influence (N. 81). The object of *parā bhakti,* then, is *Īśvara* (Ś. 2, N. 2), the Supreme Lord, Who is the origin and life of all created things, towards Whom all creation moves, and in whom everything finally disappears (*Taittirīya Upaniṣad,* III.i.1), that is, *Saguṇa* Brahman, i.e., the Personal God, in other words, Brahman manifesting its *guṇas* or attributes as the Creator and Controller of the Cosmic System, as distinguished from *Nirguṇa* Brahman i.e., the Impersonal God, in other words. Brahman with its attributes in a quiescent state; for, evidently *Nirguṇa* Brahman can by no means become an object of worship and devotion. But, still, another difficulty here presents itself. Even *Saguṇa* Brahman, as such, is far above the power of comprehension of ordinary mortals; how then, are they to cultivate devotion towards Him? It is by worshipping Him first in His sensible forms, i.e., as mainfested in Creation, for He is the *virāṭātmā,* the Soul of this grand and glorious system of the universe, *viśvarūpa*, of Whom the universe is the outward form. For, as explained by Rāmānuja in the *Śrībhāṣya* the highest Brahman called Vāsudeva, from kindness to those devoted to it, voluntarily abides in a fourfold form (i.e., Vāsudeva Saṅkarṣaṇa, Pradyumna and Aniruddha), so as to render itself accessible to its devotees. Accordingly Śāṇḍilya teaches that the World and the Object of Worship are not two different things, inasmuch as He is the inner essence, *svarūpa*, the very Self, of all things (Ś. 85). This, however, does not necessarily involve pantheism in its bad sense; for while God is immanent in the World, He at the same time also transcends it, as Lord Kṛṣṇa declares in the *Gītā* (X.42): "I stand, pervading this entire universe by a part Me." But the easier and more attractive form of the worship of *Saguṇa* Brahman is worship of Him in His Incarnations. *Parā bhakti* may be cultivated towards the Incarnation also (Ś. 46). An 'Incarnation of Brahman', however, is not a mere figment of the imagination; for, the Lord Himself declares in the *Gītā* (IV.9), that He undergoes birth and activity in the midst of mortals. But His birth is a divine event, being due solely to His own Energy (Ś. 48). Says the Lord also: "Although I am the Unborn, and of immutable, essence, although I am the Lord of the created beings, I enter into My *Prakṛti,*—put forth My Energy,—and come into (finite) existence from age to age" (*Gītā,* IV.6). Incarnation, again, is entirely an act of compassion on His part; and compassion is a pure, unselfish attribute in Him (Ś. 49). For, the purpose of divine incarnation is thus declared in the *Gītā*: "I create Myself, O Bhārata, whenever there is decline of *dharma* or Righteousness, and rise of *a-dharma* or unrighteousness. For the protection of the virtuous and for the destruction of the wicked, and for the purpose of the establishment of *dharma,* I come into (finite) existence, from age to age, by means of My *māyā*" (IV.7 and 8). Incarnations should be, however, distinguished from the *vibhūti* or glories of the Lord. All excellences, e.g., of truth, beauty, love, power, greatness, etc., wherever found, are glories of the Lord; and an account of these glories is given in the *Gītā,* X.19-42. But *mukti* will not result from the worship of any of these glories (Ś. 50 and 51). It may be urged that whereas Vāsudeva, Kṛṣṇa, is also enumerated in the above portion of the *Gītā* as a *vibhūti* or glory of the Lord, worship of Him, therefore, will not bring about *mukti*; but this is not the case, as there is sufficient evidence that Vāsudeva's is a mere form, while Kṛṣṇa is the Lord Himself (Ś. 52 and 53). The inclusion of Vāsudeva amongst the *vibhūtis* is intended to show that He is the greatest amongst the *vṛṣṇis* (Ś. 54). Devotion to the Lord Kṛṣṇa will, therefore, lead to Release. So also will do Devotion to the other well-known Incarnations in the forms of Nṛsiṃha, Vāmana, Rāma, Buddha, etc. (Ś. 55).

IV. *The Culture of Devotion*

According to some, *jñāna* or Knowledge is instrumental in the production of *bhakti* (N. 28), while others say that they are mutually dependent (N. 29). But the teaching of Nārada is that *bhakti* is the fruit or result of itself (N. 30). Nevertheless there are several auxiliary causes to it. Thus, *bhakti* arises from the giving up of the objects of the senses and of attachment to them (N. 35), from constant worship (N. 36), from listening to, and singing, the glories of the Lord in the assemblies of men (N. 37). But principally it is obtained through the kindness of the great ones, i.e., the successful devotees, or through the touch of divine compassion (N. 38). Companionship of the great, however, is difficult to obtain (N. 39). It can be obtained only through the mercy of God (N. 40), inasmuch as there is no difference between God and His good men (N. 41). Evil company should be forsaken by all means (N. 42), as it is the cause of lust, resentment, bewilderment, lapse of memory, loss of understanding, loss of everything (N. 44). These evil tendencies, ordinarily playing in ripples under the breeze of *māyā,* behave like the sea by association with the whrilwind of evil company (N. 45). Who crosses over *māya*? It is he who avoids evil company, attends upon men of large hearts, and becomes selfless (N. 46),—who retires into solitude, roots out all worldly attachments, does not yield to the influences of the three *guṇas, sattva, rajas* and *tamas,* and gives up both acquisition and preservation (N. 47), who renounces the results of his action, consecrates all action to God, and thereby rises above the influence of contraries such as pleasure and pain, heat and cold (N. 48),—who puts aside the Vedas also, and acquires pure, uninterrupted attachment to the Lord (N. 49). He not only himself crosses over *māyā,* but also helps to cross over their *māyā* (N. 50). The aspirant should not listen to talks about women, wealth, and the conduct of atheists (N. 63). He should give up egotism, pride, etc. (N. 64). Having consecrated all conduct to the Lord, he should make Him the object of his lust, resentment, pride, etc. (N. 65). Argumentation about God and about devotion to Him must not be undertaken (N. 74), as there is room for error and uncertainty in it (N. 75). *Bhaktiśāstra*, Teachings on Devotion, should be studied intelligently, and observances enjoined therein should be performed (N. 76). Much of our time, short as it is, is taken up with the experiences of pleasure, pain, desire, gain, and the like; not a single moment even of the little that is left, which, as it were, waits for attention to them, should be passed in vain (N. 77). Harmlessness, truthfulness, purity, kindness, faith, and other excellences of character should be observed (N. 78). And after all the Lord alone should be worshipped at all times with the whole heart and in faithful spirit (N. 79). For, being invoked, He at once reveals Himself, and fills His devotees with His influence (N. 80) as, with Him, it is *bhakti*, that carries the greatest weight (N. 81).

Now, *parā bhakti, parama prema,* Supreme Love, is the primary object to which the devotee aspires. There are eighty-one minor forms of devotion which lead up to it. They are collectively called *gauṇī bhakti* or secondary Devotion. The question may arise whether these lower stages of Devotion have to be cultivated simultaneously, successively, or alternatively. To this Śāṇḍilya gives the reply that there is no hard and fast rule for the application of these subsidiary means, but that their application depends upon the requirements of each particular case, like the use of various materials in the construction and repair of a building (Ś. 62); for everyone of them is capable of pleasing the Lord (Ś. 62); for everyone of them is capable of pleasing the Lord (Ś. 63), and thereby leading to *parā bhakti.*

We trace here, in broad outline, the progress of a *saṃsārī jīva* towards *mukti* along the path of *bhakti*. Experience of pleasure and pain is a fundamental fact of human existence. It falls to the lot of every mortal. But it is the fortunate few who can realize the significance of it. If the *jīva* has acquired *sukṛta* or merits in his previous birth and if he is discriminative, the experience of pleasure and pain in unending alternation will produce a feeling of dissatisfaction and disgust in him and will awaken him to the utter helplessness of his situation. Thereafter will dawn in him *śraddhā*, faith, namely, the belief that there is a moral Governor of the World, who rules the destinies of the *jīvas* according to immutable laws. Here, for the first time, is made differentiation between the Here and the Hereafter. This is the moment of the birth of Religion. Now the *jīva* avoids waste of energy in useless, though, it may be, harmless, pursuits (*aśāstra-tyāga*), and confines his activities within the code of morality (*śāstra*) which regulates conduct by means of which the Supreme Good may be attained. Gradually he forbears more and more from doing prohibited acts, and pays ever-increasing attention to the performance of acts prescribed. At the same time he learns to put out *abhimāna* or Self-assumption, i.e., to perform acts not for the sake of the fruits which they may produce, but in a spirit of devotion to duty. Thus *karma yoga,* the Path of Action, ends in the purification of the mind of *abhimāna*. This may be said to be the first stage of devotional self-culture. The second stage begins with the feeling of the necessity of some *sādhana* or means of Release. Such a means can be found in the company of *sādhus* or pious men. The aspirant, therefore, should keep company with the *sādhus* and render service unto them. *Sādhu-sevā*, to serve pious men, is the first act of worship, wherein lies the Seed of Divine Love. Companionship of the *sādhus* and *sādhu-sevā* will produce a little indifference to worldly objects, and attachment to the things of the other world. Next will follow occasional contemplation mixed with extraneous thoughts. This impurity of extraneous thoughts is due to what is called *anartha* or evils. *Anartha* is fourfold, according as it arises from (1) *duṣkṛta*, demerits, (2) *sukṛta,* merits, (3) *aparādha,* failings or faults, and (4) *bhakti,* devotion. They are called *anartha* or evils, because they cause distraction. *Aparādha,* faults, may be of ten kinds: (a) to speak evil of the Vaiṣṇavas, (b) to treat Śiva and Viṣṇu and different deities, (c) to look upon guru, religious preceptor, as an ordinary mortal, (d) to disparage the *śāstras,* codes of mortality, (e) to regard the powers attributed to the singing of the names of the Lord as mere puffs, (f) to put wrong or far-fetched construction upon the name of the Lord, (g) to do sinful acts thinking that the power of the name will save the sinner, (h) to treat the name as of equal potency with any other virtuous act, (i) to teach the name to unbelievers, and (j) to learn the power of the name and yet not to be attracted to it. *Aparādhas* arising from *bhakti* are such as the desire for worldly gain, reputation and the like, which may be easily acquired through devotion. All this impurity will be, however, washed away by *jñāna yoga*, Reflection upon the Self or Realization of the Self in thought, listening to, and signing, the names and achievements (*līlā*) of the Lord, and other means such as mentioned above. And the result will be growing steadiness of contemplation, and constancy in worship. Constancy in worship (*niṣṭhā*) will give rise to *ruci* or feeling of enjoyment, or intellectual relish, of the life of devotion, and *ruci* will be followed by *āsakti* or attachment and consequent depth of contemplation. *Āsakti* may be induced either by the perception of *aiśvarya* or the majesty and lordliness of God, or by the perception of *mādhurya* or the grace and beauty of God. The former is called *guṇa* (attribute) *māhātmya* (majesty) *āsakti* (attachment), and the latter is called *rūpa* (grace and beauty) *āsakti* (attachment). These are followed by *pūjā āsakti* or attachment to worship. In these forms of attachment the devotee is possessed with the sentiment of awe and wonder, and stands, as it were, at some distance from the Lord, feeling his own insignificance and sinfulness on the one hand, and the majesty and holiness of the Lord on the other. But the influence of Love is at work, and, after the intermediate stage of *smaraṇa āsakti* or attachment in the form of constantly recurring thinking about the Lord, there succeeds attachment in the forms of closer and closer personal relationship. The first of them to evolve is *dāsya* (service) *āsakti* (attachment). The devotee becomes attached in rendering service to the Lord, as a servant does to his master. *Dāsya āsakti* into *sakhya* (friendship) *āsakti* (attachment). The devotee becomes attached to the Lord, as is one to one's friend. *Sakhya āsakti* evolves into *vātsalya* (parental love) *āsakti* (attachment). The devotee becomes attached to the Lord, as is a father to his son. And *vātsalya āsakti* evolves into *kāntā* (wife) *āsakti* (attachment). The devotee becomes attached to the Lord, as is a faithful wife to her husband. But the personal element also has to be dropped before the next higher stage can be reached; and, thus, the fulfilment or *kāntā āsakti*, whether it be conversant about the *aiśvarya* or the *mādhurya* of the Lord, is in *ātma* (self) *nivedana* (dedication) *āsakti* (attachment), when the devotee sacrifices himself to the Lord, completely identifies his will with His will, loses his separate existence in the wider existence of the Lord. Thereafter he attains to the state of *tanmaya* (absorption in Him) *āsakti* (attachment), that is, of absolute self-forgetfulness. This is called *bhāva*, trance, *samādhi,* deep meditation, wherein there takes place manifestation of the Supreme Being. This is the sprouting stage of divine love. *Bhāva* then grows into *mahā bhāva*, the higher trance, which is the state of *parama* (extreme) *viraha* (separation) *āsakti* (attachment). As in the case of true lovers during separation, so here also the devotee becomes mad after God, realizes. His presence within himself as well as outside him, and verily lives, moves and has his being in Him. This is *parama prema*, the consummation of Love. Hereby the knot of the heart (*hṛdaya-granthi*), which binds the *jīva* to the *saṃsāra,* is cut asunder, all doubt is set at rest, and *karma,* the cause of re-birth, is exhausted. Thus the *jīva* overcomes *māyā,* and obtains Release. If it happens during life, he is called *jīvan-mukta*, living yet released; if after death, he is then called *videha mukta*, disembodied and released.

V. *The Forms and Expressions of Devotion*

Devotion is indicated by (a) *sammāna,* honour, as in the case of Arjuna, (b) *vahumāna*, exaltation, as in the case of Ikṣvāku (*Nṛsiṃha Purāṇa*, XXV.22), (c) *prīti,* pleasure, as in the case of Vidura (*Mahābhārata,* Udyoga Parva, LXXXIX.24), (d) *viraha*, (pangs of) separation, as in the case of the *gopīs* (*Viṣṇu Purāṇa,* V.xviii.17), (e) *itara-vicikitsā*, disinclination to others, as in the case of Upamanyu (*Mahābhārata*, Anuśāsana Parva, XIV.186), (f) *mahimā-khyāti*, glorification, as in the case of Yama (*Viṣṇu Purāṇa*, III.vii.10), (g) *tadartha prāṇa sthāna,* living for Him, as in the case of Hanumān (*Rāmāyaṇa,* Uttara Kāṇḍa, CVII. 31), (h) *tadiyatā*, the belief that everything belongs to Him, as in the case of Uparicara Vasu (*Mahābhārata,* Śānti Parva, chaps. 336-37), (i) *sarva-tad-bhāva*, the consciousness that He is immanent in all things, as in the case of Prahlāda (*Viṣṇu Purāṇa*, I.xix.5), (j) *a-prātikūlya*, non-opposition, as in the case of Bhīṣma (*Mahābhārata,* Bhīṣma Parva, LIX.97), and the like (Ś. 44, N. 19), such as ardour in worship, and in constant talk about Him (N. 16-18).

Before we proceed to describe the various forms of Devotion, we should better explain the statement we have made above, namely, that there are eighty-one varieties of it. And for this purpose we make the following quotation from the gloss of Ācārya Śrīdhara on the *Śrīmad Bhāgavatam*, III.xxix.8, 9, 10, 11: "Thus *tāmasa,* and the other (viz., *rājasa* and *sāttvika*) forms of devotion contain three varieties each, of which superiority belongs to each succeeding one. Accordingly *śravaṇa* (listening to talks and songs about the Lord), *kīrtana,* singing songs about

Him, etc. viz., *smaraṇa* (constantly thinking about Him), *pāda-sevana* (doing homage to Him) *arcana* (worshipping Him), *vandana* (making obeisance to Him), *dāsya* (rendering service unto Him), *sakhya* (behaving like a friend towards Him), and *ātmanivedana* (dedicating one's self to Him), everyone of them contains nine varieties. So that *saguṇa bhakti* (vide below) becomes eighty-one-fold. Whereas *nirguṇa bhakti* (vide below) is of one kind only".

Now, the means of obtaining Release is the *anuśīlana*, pursuit, of the *para-tattva,* Supreme Reality, Śrī Kṛṣna, the Lord, and He may be pursued from various motives. For example, addressing Yudhiṣṭhira, Nārada says: "By fixing their minds of *Īśvara*, through love, through hate, through fear, through friendship, as by devotion, and thereby avoiding their sins, many have found access to Him; the *gopīs* through love, Kaṃsa through fear, Śiśupāla and other rulers of men through hate, the Vṛṣṇis through relationship, you (i.e., Yudhiṣṭhira), O great one, through friendship, we by devotion." (Vide *Śrīmadbhāgavatam*, VII.i.29, 30). It is also stated in ibid., 26, "My (i.e., Narada's, firm belief is that a mortal cannot attain *tanmayatā*, absorption into Him, the sense of His over-bearing presence everywhere, transformation into Him in thought, so easily by the practice of devotion as by perseverance in hostility (towards Him)." Broadly speaking, therefore, it may be said that the Supreme Reality may be pursued either as an object of love or as an object of hatred, the end in view being the same in both, viz., *kena api upāyena manaḥ kṛṣṇe nivesayet*, that is, to set the mind firmly on Kṛṣṇa by whatever means (ibid., 31).

The loving pursuit of the Supreme Reality results, at its next moment, in the generation of *bhāva,* sentiment, by means of *kriyā*, the performance of operscribed acts. This *bhāva* and this *kriyā* are the rudiments of *bhakti*. At its origin *bhakti*, except in very rare cases, is *saguṇā,* modified, *sopādhi*, mixed, and it gradually evolves into the *nirguṇa nirupādhi* form, i.e., the form of *bhakti* unmodified pure and colourless, which is the immediate cause of Release. *Sopādhi bhakti*, again, is either *sakāma,* containing within it desire for objects other than the pleasure of the Lord, or *niṣkāma* motiveless. *Sakāma bhakti* is also called *guṇī-bhūta* or secondary, because in it *karma*, religious performances, *jñāna,* knowledge, and the practice of *yoga* are the principal elements, while *bhakti* is merely subsidiary to them. Its results are *siddhi,* success, that is, success in religious performances, the development of knowledge, and the practice of *yoga*, and *bhakti*, enjoyment, that is, of heaven and the like. It becomes three-fold according as it is cultivated by *ārta,* the afflicted, *jijñāsu*, the inquisitive, or *artha-arthī,* the needful. And each of these three kinds is further subdivided as *sāttvikī*, white, *rājasī*, red, and *tāmasī*, black, according as the principles of *sattva, rajas*, and *tamas*, or illumination, attraction, and ignorance are dominant in them (Cf. *Gītā*, chap. XVII). *Niṣkāma bhakti* is also called *pradhānībhūta*, or primary, because in it *bhakti* is the principal element, although it is intermixed with *karma, jñāna*, or *yoga*. Only the wise are competent for the cultivation of it (Cf. *Gītā*, VII.16). *Niṣkāma bhakti*, associated with religious performances, consists in *karma-kāraṇa*, performance of duties, and *phala-arpaṇa*, dedication of the consequences thereof to God. This is *karma yoga*, the Path of Action, the result of which is *cittaśuddhi*, purification of the mind. It is called *āropa-siddhā bhakti*, i.e., *bhakti* by attribution, inasmuch as purification of mind being also producible by *bhakti, karma* is here attributed as *bhakti*. By means of purification of mind, it leads to the growth or *jñāna-miśrā* and *yoga-miśrā bhakti*, i.e., those forms of *niṣkāma bhakti* in which development of knowledge and practice of *yoga* play are important part. These forms of *bhakti* are known as *saṅga-siddhā bhakti, bhakti* by association, inasmuch as spiritual cognition constituting development of knowledge, and spiritual practices constituting *yoga*, by operating along with *bhakti*, lead to *parama-ātma-sākṣātkāra*, Spiritual Intuition of the Supreme Self, which is the proper function of *bhakti*. The cultivation of *niṣkāma bhakti* attended with *jñāna*, constitutes *jñana yoga*, the Path of Knowledge. Its result is *sadyaḥ-mukti*, immediate release, by means of *brahma-jñāna*, knowledge of Brahman. *Niṣkāma bhakti* attended with *yoga*, is known as *aṣṭāṅga-yoga*, the eight-limbed *yoga*. Its result is *krama-mukti*, gradual release. Thus *jñāna* and yoga become means of release only when they are attended with *niṣkāma bhakti*. It has been accordingly taught that *bhakti*, properly so-called, i.e., *nirupādhi bhakti* (vide below), or *bhakti* pure and colourless, is superior to *karma, jñāna*, and *yoga* (N. 25-27, 58-60; Ś. 22, 23). These various forms of *bhakti* are characterised as *aparā*, the lower, as distinguished from *nirupādhi bhakti* which is called *parā*, the higher, and to which *aparā bhakti* is subsidiary (N. 56; Ś. 56).

Nirupādhi bhakti is characterised as *uttamā*, the excellent, *kevalā* the simple *śuddhā*, the pure, and *svarūpa-siddhā* existing by itself. It is the essence of *bhakti yoga*, the Path of Devotion, and its results are *prema*, love, and *bhāgavat-sākṣātkāra*, spiritual intuition of the Lord. It is path for *sraddhālu* or the believers. *Nirupādhi bhakti* gradually evolves from *prema* or mere love to *parama-prema* or supreme love, and for its evolution depends only upon itself (N. 30); that is to say, *ceṣṭā*, exertion of body, speech, and mind, prompted by love, at a previous stage, becomes the means of its evolution into the next higher stage. These higher stages of love are of the form of *rati*, joyful attachment. *Rati*, again, is distinguished under the aspects of *bhāva,* sentiment, in which the sense of separate personality still remains, and *prema,* love, in which the sense of separate personality gardually disappears altogether. *Rati* under the aspect of *bhāva* successively evolves as *guṇa-māhātmya-āsakti,* attachment to the attributes and greatness of the Lord, *rūpa-āsakti*, attachment to the beauty of the Lord, *pūjā-āsakti*, attachment to the worship of the Lord, and *smaraṇa-āsakti*, attachment to constant thinking about the Lord. In them, it will be observed, the distance between the devotee and the Lord gradually diminishes, but nevertheless no personal relationship is established between them. That takes palce in *rati* under the aspect of *prema.* It begins as *dāsya-āsakti*, attachment in servantship, in which appreciation of, and entire sympathy with the will of the master may not necessarily be present. These characteristics appear in the succeeding form of *prema-rati,* viz., *sakhya-āsakti* attachment in friendship, where, however, sacrifice of the will in favour of, and subordination of the will to, the will of the friend may not be present, as they are in the next succeeding form of *prema-rati*, viz., *vātsalya-āsakti*, attachment in fathership, where the father exercises self-denial for the sake of the son. This spirit of self-sacrifice goes on developing, and *vātsalya-āsakti* is followed first by *kāntā-āsakti*, attachment in wife-hood, in which the wife identifies her whole being with the being of her Lover, and then by *ātma-nivedana-āsakti*, attachment in self-consecration, wherein the spirit of self-sacrifice finds its natural fulfilment. Consequently the next higher form is that of *tat-maya-āsakti*, attachment in transformation or absorption into Him. This is *advaita-siddhi*, the perfection of monistic idealism, the realization of the great truth, namely, *vāsudevaḥ sarvam*, that all is Vāsudeva, Kṛṣna, the Supreme Reality. As attachment in this form grows deeper and deeper, it rises into, and culminates in, *parma-viraha-āsakti*, attachment in extreme separation, in which the devotee, though he is at the time permanently united with the Lord, still feels as if he were separated from Him, as, for example, described by the Vaiṣṇava poet, Govindadāsa "*rodati rādhā syāma kari kora, hari hari kāmhāgeo prāṇanātha mora*", while holding Śyāma in her arms, Rādhā still weeps, "Hari! Hari! Where is the Lord of my life gone?"

Rati under the aspect of *prema*, developing in these forms, may follow *vidhi-mārga*, the path of the performance of duty, or *rāga-mārga*, the path of attraction to the Lord. The former leads to the enjoyment of the *aiśvarya* or the lordliness of God, and is, therefore, *miśrā* or mixed, while the latter causes the enjoyment of the *mādhurya* or sweetness of the beauty of the

Lord, and is, therefore, *kevalā* or pure. It is pure *prema-rati*, called by Nārada *parama-prema* or Supreme Love, which is the consummation of Devotional Self-Culture, and the immediate cause of release.

VI. *What is the Nature of Devotion*?

Higher Devotion consists in attachment to *Īśvara* (Ś. 2). It is of the form of *parama-prema* or intense love towards Him (N. 2), and is the source of eternal freedom from the coil of mortality (N. 2); by obtaining which man becomes perfected, becomes immortal, becomes satisfied (N. 4); by attaining which he desires nothing else, grieves not, hates not, revels not, seeks nothing else (N. 5); by knowing which he becomes mad, becomes still, becomes self-satisfied (N. 6). It contains no worldly desires within itself; on the contrary, it arises on the inhibition of all worldly desires (N. 7-14). Sometimes it appears by itself in a fit receptacle (N. 53). The nature of *parama-prema*, however, cannot be described in words (N. 51), like the nature of taste felt by a dumb person (N. 52). It is attributeless, desireless, swelling up more and more at every moment, flowing incessantly, in the form of subtler feeling (N. 54), and transforming all objects of seeing, hearing, and thinking into itself (N. 55).

न धनं न जनं सुन्दरीं कवितां वा जगदीश कामये।
मम जन्मनि जन्मनीश्वरे भवताद्भक्तिरहैतुकी त्वयि।।

I crave not for money, nor for men, nor for a beautiful woman, nor for poetic genius, O Lord of the World; in every birth of mine may *ahaituki bhakti*, spontaneous devotion, grow in me towards Thee, the Lord.—Śrī Caitanya

Bhaktisūtras

अथातो भक्तिं व्याख्यास्यामः ।। १ ।।

अथ (*atha*), this word may be taken as benedictory or as merely introducing the subject. अतः (*ataḥ*) hence, therefore; because knowledge or apprehension of truth and right conduct are not in themselves sufficient to bring about salvation, but, for this, must be leavened with the enthusiasm of devotion. भक्तिं (*bhaktiṃ*), (the doctrine of) devotion. व्याख्यास्यामः (*vyākhyāsyāmaḥ*), (we) shall expound.

1. Now, therefore, we shall expound the doctrine of devotion.

Note: The philosophy of Devotion by Śaṇḍilya begins thus: "Now, therefore, inquiry into Devotion."

Note: But it might be at once said that the devotion which is here sought to supplement thought and action, is not an altogether unknown thing and it might as well be doubted if it will after all solve the great problem of human existence, namely, the liberation of the soul from the coil of mortality. In fact, in their social and domestic relations men have had experience of the delightful influence of affection, love, admiration, reverence, and similar other sentiments. But nobody considers this to be adequate for the supreme purpose of life. All this is, however, admitted. At the same time it is maintained that although there certainly is not any difference of kind between devotion, on the one hand, and other cognate sentiments, on the other, still there is perceptibly a difference of degree between them. While these various modes of feeling are but developments of the root principle of sympathetic response of the human heart to congenial excitations from the outside, devotion is the consummation of them all. Further, we notice another very important characteristic of devotion. The object of all attachment on earth is perishable, and, therefore, finite; whereas devotion aspires to something imperishable and infinite. It is only when the soul catches faint glimpses of the divine in nature, within or around itself, that it is seized with the all-consuming enthusiasm of devotion, and forgetting and forsaking everything else, strives to throw itself entirely at the service of its God and its Lord, in which service its satisfaction is infinite.

These two points are made clear in the next aphorism which describes what devotion is.

सा त्वस्मिन् परमप्रेमरूपा ।।२।।

सा (*sa*), it, devotion. तु (*tu*), but. This is in reply to the doubt referred to above in the notes. अस्मिन् (*asmin*), in or to him. Instead of this some read तस्मिन् or अस्मै. The sense is, in every case, the same, but the reading in the text gives the complete meaning, indicating that God is always near to the (*jīva*). परम (*parama*), intense. This word is intended to convey three ideas: (1) Devotion is essentially undivided, that is to say, it turns away from everything except God. (2) It is never over-shadowed by thought and action. It is itself the end. (3) It is not inert or idle. It invariably manifests itself in word, deed and thought. प्रेम (*prema*), love. रूपा (*rūpā*), form.

2. It is of the form of intense love towards Him.

Cf. Sāṇḍilya's definition of *bhakti*, "as absolute attachment to God."

Note: This devotional love comes as the climax of a course of evolution Śrīrūpa Gosvāmī, in his *Bhaktirasāmṛtasindhu*, thus traces the development of love in the case of aspirants—

"First arises faith; then follow attraction, and, after that, adoration. Adoration leads to suppression of worldly desires; and the result is single-mindedness and satisfaction. Then grows attachment which results in ebullition of sentiment. After this love comes into play."

अमृतस्वरूपा च ।।३।।

अमृतस्वरूपा (*amṛta-svarūpā*) of the nature of nectar. Like the reputed nectar, devotion once for all puts a stop to all painful and unpleasant contingencies of life, and ultimately secures freedom from the wheel of births and deaths. च (*ca*), and.

3. And it is of the nature of nectar.

Note: Śāṇḍilya also says that "it has been taught that he attains liberation, who becomes steady in devotion."

And in *Śrīmadbhāgavatam,* III. 25.38, it is said that those who run after God, never perish, and that the wheel of the wakeful God, Yama, the God of Death, does not strike them who regard God as their dear self, son, friend, preceptor, benefactor, and the chosen deity.

Read also ibid., X. 82.44 where Lord Krṣṇa says: Devotion to Me works for the immortality of beings.

In a similar strain sings Jalaluddin Rumi the great Persian poet—

"I died as mineral and became a plant,
I died as plant and rose to animal,
I died as animal and I was man.
Why should I fear? When was I less by dying?
Yet once more I shall die as man, to soar
With angels blest; but even from angelhood
I must pass on: all except God doth perish.
When I have sacrificed my angel soul,
I shall become what no mind e'er conceived.
Oh, let me not exist! for Non-existence
Proclaims in organ tones, 'To him we shall return'."

The idea in the above two aphorisms is elaborated in the three following:

यल्लब्ध्वा पुमान् सिद्धो भवत्यमृतो भवति तृप्तो भवति।।४।।

यत् (*yat*), which, love of God. लब्ध्वा (*labdhvā*), attaining. पुमान् (*pumān*), man. सिद्धः (*siddhaḥ*), successful. अमृतः (*amṛtaḥ*), immortal. तृप्तः (*tṛptaḥ*), satisfied. भवति (*bhavati*), becomes.

4. By attaining which man becomes successful, immortal, and satisfied.

This aphorism calls to mind *Gītā,* IX.31. "Before long he becomes of virtuous soul and always enjoys peace. Know for certain, O Son of Kuntī, My devotee never perishes."

यत् प्राप्य न किञ्चिद् वाञ्छति न शोचति
न द्वेष्टि न रमते नोत्साही भवति।।५।।

यत् (*yat*), which, Love of God. प्राप्य (*prāpya*), obtaining. न (*na*) not. किंचित् (*kiñcit*), anything. वांछति (*vāñchati*), desires. शोचति (*śocati*), laments. द्वेष्टि (*dveṣṭi*), loathes. रमते (*ramate*), revels. उत्साही (*utsāhī*), zealous. भवति (*bhavati*), becomes.

5. On obtaining which he does not desire anything, laments or loathes nothing, revels not, nor becomes zealous.

"Love," says Jalāluddīn, "is the remedy of our pride and self-conceit, the physician of all our infirmities. Only he whose garment is rent by love becomes entirely unselfish."

Having once found and loved God, man desires nothing else to strive after, or to avoid, or to take delight in. Herein devotion is higher than action. Not only so; it is also higher than thought. Thus—

यज्ज्ञात्वो मत्तो भवति स्तब्धो भवत्यात्मारामो भवति ।। ६ ।।

यत् (*yat*) which, Love of God. ज्ञात्वा (*jñātvā*), knowing. मत्तः (*mattaḥ*), overjoyed, mad. स्तब्धः (*stabdhaḥ*), quiet, still. आत्मारामः (*ātmārāmaḥ*), self-satisfied, One whose soul is one's best place of rest. भवति (*bhavati*), becomes.

6. By knowing which, he becomes overjoyed, quiet, and self-satisfied.

Note: It may be thought that these high characteristics are not necessarily involved in the idea of devotion. For, devotion is not after all as absolutely selfless and colourless as it should be. Love of God, the pleasing of the Lord, is the object which the devotee seems constantly to have in view. Thus, instead of welling up spontaneously from within, the flow of devotion is directed by an external influence. This, however, is not the case. No doubt the grace of God is an invariable accompaniment of the playful course of devotion within the soul, but, merely on this account, the one can hardly be posited as the cause, and the other, as the consequence. On the contrary, devotion is its own end. That the grace of God courses along with the stream of devotion, is perfectly natural. Immediately as the flower blossoms forth, it cannot but gladden the heart of the beholder. But it will not be correct to say on that score that the flower blooms to beauty with the object of pleasing man. It merely progresses a stage higher in the scale of its natural development. Similarly with devotion.

This is the text of the next aphorism.

सा न कामयमानां निरोधरूपत्वात् ।। ७ ।।

सा (*sā*), it. निरोधरूपत्वात् (*nirodha-rūpatvāt*), because of its nature as appearing in the form of suppression (of all desires) निरोध is fully explained in the following aphorisms. कामयमाना (*kāmayamānā*), selfish. Moved by desire. न (*na*), not.

7. It is not led by desire, because it finds expression in (the) inhibition (of all desires).

The "inhibition of all desires" is very often misunderstood to signify a total annihilation or extinction of all activity. This is not only absurd but is simply unworthy of man. This misunderstanding is cleared up in the next aphorism.

निरोधस्तु लोकवेदव्यापारस्यन्यासः ।। ८ ।।

तु (*tu*), on the contrary. निरोधः (*nirodhaḥ*), inhibition of desires.

लोकवेदव्यापारस्य (*loka-veda-vyāpārasya*), of customary, and scriptural observances. न्यासः (*nyāsaḥ*), resignation or consecration to the Supreme. Cf. *Gītā*, XVIII. 2. "The wise describe resignation as the giving up of the fruits of all actions."

8. On the contrary, "inhibition of desires" means the consecration of all customary and scriptural observances to the Supreme.

For the full comprehension of the import of this aphorism we may cite *Gītā*, IX.27 and 34. "Whatever thou doest, whatever thou livest upon, whatever sacrifices and gifts thou makest, and whatever penances thou practisest, O son of Kuntī, surrender all that unto Me." "Set thy mind on Me, devote thyself to Me, offer sacrifices unto Me, bow to Me, make Me thy last resort. Thus attaching thy soul to Me, thou shalt come to Me;" and also XII.6 and 7, "O Pārtha, ere long I deliver from the sea of the mortal world those who have their minds upon Me and who, surrendering, all and sundry actions unto Me, run after Me and worship and meditate upon Me with undivided concentration of mind." Evidently, therefore, instead of suggesting a cessation of activity, "inhibition of desires" implies the full and uniform direction of all thought and action towards God.

And not only this, it has a negative aspect also, Thus—

तस्मिन् अनन्यता तद्विरोधिषुदासीनता च ।। ९ ।।

तस्मिन् (*tasmin*), in him. अनन्यता (*ananyatā*), single-heartedness. तद्विरोधिषु (*tad-virodhiṣu*), in all that is antagonistic to Him. उदासीनता (*udāsīnatā*), indifference, apathy. च (*ca*), and.

9. (Inhibition also means) single-heartedness towards Him and indifference to all that is antagonistic to Him.

Now, single-heartedness as an important element in devotion cannot be a mere blind passion or a narrow prejudice. It should be arrived at as the result of a process of conscious discrimination between the passing and the permanent, in which the finites naturally come to be eliminated one by one. Hence—

अन्याश्रयाणां त्यागोऽनन्यता ।। १० ।।

अन्याश्रयाणां (*anyāśrayāṇāṃ*), of all other supports. त्यागः (*tyāgaḥ*), renunciation, giving up. अनन्यता (*ananyatā*), single-heartedness.

10. Single-heartedness (implies) the giving up of all other supports.

The cultivation of devotion may be disturbed by the operation of the various influences to which human life is every moment exposed. To restore equilibrium, the devotee should on no account seek the help of other instruments than those employed in the cultivation of devotion itself, namely, listening to talks about the Lord, singing His name, and so forth.

लोकवेदेषु तदनुकूलाचरणं तद्विरोधिषूदासीनता ।। ११ ।।

लोकवेदेषु (*loka-vedeṣu*). In respect of social and religious ordinances. तदनुकूलाचरणं (*tad-anukūla-ācaraṇam*), practice or performance which is congenial to Him. अनुकूल, however, must be taken in a relative sense. Not that there are particular injunctions which are specially favoured by the deity; but ordinances, social or scriptural, as such, are prescribed in general terms for a large assembly of human beings who, amongst themselves, are in different stages of development and degrees of potentiality. Hence the question should be decided, in each individual case, with reference only to the would-be agent's environment, inherited and acquired capabilities, temperament, and so on. तद्विरोधिषूदासीनता (*tad-virodhiṣu-udāsīnatā*), indifference to all that conflicts with Him.

11. By "indifference to all that conflicts with Him" (Ś. 9) is understood the performance of those social and scriptural rites and ceremonies which are congenial to Him.

In the eighth aphorism we have been taught to direct all our energies of thought and action towards God. Now we are again enjoined to respect to some extent, the dictates of religion and morality. Here seems, therefore, to arise some confusion which is, however, only superficial. The due practice, of moral and religious ordinances involves, in most cases, a large amount of bodily distress and tension of mind and an altogether indefinite abstinences from the joys of life. This, then, is unsupportable on merely selfish notions, however, strong and alluring these may, at first, appear to be. It becomes possible only when the inner vision, rising above the narrow limitations of its immediate surroundings, comes to look upon a 'far-off divine thing'. Except in such happy circumstances, the observance of rites and ceremonies really comes to nothing, as Lord Kṛṣṇa declares in *Gītā*, XVII.27-28—"Performance of sacrifices, penances and charities is also said to endure as well as action which is done for His sake. (Whereas) offerings made unto fire, gifts given, penances practised, and duty done, without belief (in the existence of a divine Providence), is said not to endure. O Pārtha, that avails neither here nor elsewhere."

To this the inquisitive aspirant may justly reply that once "the vision beatific" is realised, there seems to be left no room for pious observances.

For, these are prescribed simply for the purpose of purifying the mirror of the mind in which the Oversoul may then, and only then, cast its reflection in all its shades and lineaments. Quite so, but this is so in exceptional cases only. Ordinarily, however, there is some need for the performance of rites and ceremonies, as will be evident from the next two aphorisms. We shall moreover do well to bear in mind that these two things, namely, faith in God and observance of sacred laws and customs, are mutually involved, and that they in turn act and react upon each other in the continuous process of gradual development of devotional life.

भवतु निश्चयदाढ्र्यादूर्ध्वं शास्त्ररक्षणम् ।। १२ ।।

निश्चयदाढ्र्यात् (*niścaya-dārḍhyāt*), after the deepening of faith (in God), cf. *Bhaktiratnāvalī*, IV.36. ऊर्ध्वं (*ūrddhvaṃ*), above, after. शास्त्ररक्षणं (*śāstrarakṣaṇaṃ*), observance of sacred laws. भवतु (*bhavatu*), let there be.

12. The observance of the sacred laws may be continued after the deepening of faith in God.

In the *Bhaktirasāmṛtasindhu* it has been observed that "the aspirant who takes to devotion with an object (see *infra*, aphorism 56) requires to abide by the scriptures and favourable maxims, till the ebullition of sentiment" which is called Love. St. Paul also says: "If ye are led by the Spirit, ye are not under the law." "In the lower stages of meditation," says St. Theresa, "the setting aside of material images should not be attempted before the soul is very far advanced, as it is clear that till then it ought to seek the Creator by means of creatures. To do otherwise is to act as if we were angels." St. Gregory the Great has said: "If we wish to reach the citadel of contemplation, we must begin by exercising ourselves in the field of labour. Whoever wishes to give himself to contemplation must first examine what degree of love he is capable of; for love is the lever of the soul. It alone is able to detach it from this world and give it wings."

अन्यथा पातित्यशङ्कया ।। १३ ।।

अन्यथा (*anyathā*), otherwise. पातित्यशङ्कया (*pātityaśaṅkayā*), for fear of fall.

13. (The sacred laws should be observed even after faith in God has deepened), lest, otherwise, there may be a fall.

Some interpret the aphorsim to mean: "The sacred laws must be observed, till faith in God becomes deepened; for, otherwise, there is fear of a fall."

Well, then, it is understood that our only concern should be to hold up God as our utmost all, to consecrate ourselves, body and soul, to His service, and never to allow worldly desires and pursuits to distract and divert the even flow of a career of piety and devotion. To this high end we may even dispense with the regular observance of sacred practices after our faith in God has become firm and fixed. That their performance may still be continued is a matter of convenience and caution merely.

And, it goes without saying that humdrum routine of the ordinary life may be also safely neglected. But nevertheless, as we are, we cannot sufficiently devote ourselves to the service of God, for there seems to be no escape from a totally different kind of distraction, namely, the perpetual thought for our backs and bellies. It is, then, seriously suggested that we should take no care of our bodies, but instead leave them to their own fate? Not at all. We can never lose sight of the fact so graphically stated by Kālidāsa that शरीरमाद्यं खलु धर्म्मसाधनम्, the body is verily the primary requisite for the cultivation of virtue. But this consideration, instead of causing distraction, fastens our attention all the more upon God in whose service we seek to live, move and have our being. St. Francis of Assisi used to say: "We must needs use great discretion in the way we treat our brother, the body, if we would not have it excite in us a storn of melancholy."

Therefore in the next aphorism we have—

लोकोऽपितावदेव भोजनादिव्यापारस्त्वाशरीरधारणावधि ।। १४ ।।

लोकः (*lokaḥ*), social customs and usages. अपि (*api*), also. तावत् (*tāvat*), to that extent. एव (*eva*), only. भोजनादिव्यापारः (*bhojana-ādi-vyāpāraḥ*), the occupation of eating, drinking, dressing, etc. तु (*tu*), on the other hand. आशरीरधारणावधि (*ā-śarīra-dhāraṇāvadhi*), to the end of the carrying of the body.

14. Social customs and usages also are to be observed only to the same extent (as scriptural ordinances). But, on the other hand, the occupation of eating, drinking, dressing, and so on, should be continued so long as we have to carry the physical organism.

The purport of the above three aphorisms is this—The consciousness of God, which is innate in every soul, should be first developed and strengthened by considerations of theology, which is an enquiry into the existence and attributes of God and His relation to Man and the World. It is only then that a man acquires strength of mind enough to observe the scriptural and customary ordinances in their true spirit. The result of this life of holiness and piety is that, besides knowing God, he now comes to love Him and to realize his fellowship with Him. At this stage, when his will has taken a wholly moral and religious turn, he can safely dispense with the scriptural and customary injunctions, since piety has come to be a rule of life and a labour of love to him. But he will have to take care of his body as long as he lives.

तल्लक्षणानि वाच्यन्ते नानामतभेदात् । । १५ । ।

तल्लक्षणानि (*tal-lakṣaṇāni*), marks or indications of devotion. नानामतभेदात् (*nānā-mata-bhedāt*), according to diverse opinions. वाच्यन्ते (*vācyante*), are being stated.

15. The marks of devotion are now being stated according to diverse opinions.

Thinkers agree as to the essential character of devotion; but they give prominence to one or other of its various manifestations in order just to indicate its nature from their several points of view.

पूजादिष्वनुराग इति पाराशर्य्यः । । १६ । ।

पूजादिषु (*pūjādiṣu*), in worship and like performances. अनुराग: (*anurāgah*), attachment, ardour. इति (*iti*), thus. पाराशर्य्य: (*pārāśaryyaḥ*), the disciple of Parāśara.

16. Ardour in His worship and like performances, is the mark of devotion, according to the disciple of Parāśara.

कथादिष्विति गर्गः । । १७ । ।

कथादिषु (*kathā-ādiṣu*), in talks of His glory and greatness. इति (*iti*), thus. गर्ग: (*gargaḥ*), a sage of that name.

17. Garga thinks that application in talks of His glory and greatness is the sign of devotion.

आत्मरत्यविरोधेनेति शाण्डिल्यः । । १८ । ।

आत्मरत्यविरोधेन (*ātma-rati-avirodhena*), without hindrance to the enjoyment of bliss which the human soul finds in God or in itself. इति (*iti*), thus. शाण्डिल्य: (*śāṇḍilyaḥ*), a sage of that name.

18. The mark of devotion is ardour in His worship and indulgence in talks of His glory and greatness, provided they do not hinder the enjoyment of bliss which the soul finds in God: so says Śāṇḍilya.

Note: It will be seen, therefore, that whatever draws the mind away from God can never be favourable to the culture of devotion. On the other hand, eveything which relates to God and holds Him constantly before our mind's eye, has the effect of deepening the flow of devotion. This is the sum and substance of the above three aphorisms which are incorporated in the following one.

नारदस्तु तदर्पिताखिलाचारता तद्विस्मरणे परमव्याकुलतेति ।। १६ ।।

नारद: (*nāradaḥ*), the heavenly saint of that name, of whose composition these aphorisms are. तु (*tu*), however. तदर्पिताखिलाचारता (*tad-arpita-akhila-ācāratā*), the condition of having dedicated all observances whatsoever to Him. तद्विस्मरणे (*tad-vismaraṇe*), in losing Him from memory. परमव्याकुलता (*paramavyākulatā*), extreme uneasiness. इति (*iti*), thus.

19. Nārada thinks, however, that devotion is indicated by the condition of having dedicated all observances whatsoever to Him, and by the feeling of extreme uneasiness in losing Him from memory.

But is such a climax ever attainable? Yes, certainly. It is not at all an impracticable ideal. For—

अस्त्येवमेवम् ।। २० ।।

एवमेवम् (*evamevam*), such and such. अस्ति (*asti*), exists.

20. There are such and such instances.

यथा व्रजगोपिकानाम् ।। २१ ।।

यथा (*yathā*), as for instance. व्रजगोपिकानाम् (*vraja-gopikānām*), in the case of the cow-maids of Vraja or Vṛndāvana.

21. As, for instance, in the case or the cow-maids of Vṛndāvana (who are reported to have dedicated all their actions to Lord Kṛṣṇa and to have felt extreme uneasiness in losing Him from their midst even for a short while).

In this context the reader may, with profit, turn to chapters 29 and 30, part X, of *Śrīmadbhāgavatam.*

Now, Love certainly exercises a levelling influence. It smooths down all inequalities and brings the lover and the beloved on the same footing. And so devotion results in a fusion of personalities, leaving only the divine. It may be imagined, however, that the intimacy of love may not infrequently lead one to lose sight of the magnificence and majesty of God, which transcends all one's sublimest aspirations. This will surely be a serious drawback to reckon with in any system of religious culture. Quite so, but fortunately this does not necessarily happen. On the contrary, a full and conscious realization of the grandeur and majesty of God enhances, all the more, His supreme importance as an object of admiration and worship, in the eye of the devotee. Thus we have in the next aphorism—

तत्रापि न माहात्म्यज्ञानविस्मृत्यपवादः ।। २२ ।।

तत्र (*tatra*), there, in the absolute fusion of personalities of the human with the divine. अपि (*api*), even. माहात्म्यज्ञानविस्मृत्यपवादः (*māhātmya-jñāna-vismṛti-apavādaḥ*), particular reason for forgetting the idea of greatness (of God). न (*na*), not.

22. Even there, in the absolute fusion of personalities, there is no particular reason for forgetting the idea of the greatness of God.

The life of Lord Kṛṣṇa affords more than one illustration of the truth of this statement.

On the contray, without a vivid awareness of the majesty of God, devotion can seldom, if at all, operate as a persistent principle of spiritual development. Hence—

तद्विहीनं जाराणामिव ।। २३ ।।

तद्विहीनं (*tad-vihīnaṃ*), deprived of that. जाराणाम् (*jārāṇām*), of paramours. इव (*iva*) as.

23. Deprived of the sense of divine greatness, devotion is as the love of a woman towards her paramours (which is constantly shifting from person to person, in an indefinite manner, according as one appears more desirable than another).

Besides, it lacks another great characteristic of pure love, namely—

नास्त्येव तस्मिंस्तत्सुखसुखित्वम् ।। २४ ।।

तस्मिन् (*tasmin*), in that, therein. In illicit love. तत्सुखसुखित्वम् (*tat-sukha-sukhitvaṃ*), the feeling of happiness in the happiness of him, the paramour. न (*na*), not. अस्ति (*asti*), is, exists. एव (*eva*), certainly.

24. In illicit love there certainly exists no corresponding feeling of happiness (on the part of either) in the happiness (of the other).

It is now proposed to compare the relative usefulness and excellence of the recognised methods of realizing the supreme object of human existence, on the one side, and the doctrine of devotion on the other. It has been laid down in the *Aitareya Āraṇyaka* "एषः पन्था एतत् कर्मैतत् ब्रह्मैतत् सत्यम्"

"This is the way, this action, and this knowledge; this is true." And the erudite Sāyaṇa comments: "तत्र कर्म्मशब्देन तद्विषयज्ञानपूर्व्वकमनुष्ठानं विवचितम्। ब्रह्मशब्देन तद्विषयज्ञानमात्रम्" that is, by 'action' here is signified performance in the light of knowledge about Him, while 'knowledge' means simply to realise Him in the understanding to the utmost limit, so that on the aspirant coming to know Him in all His greatness and glory, all worldly desires may dry up within the mind which will then naturally fix upon the supremely desirable, and become absorbed in His blissful contemplation. In *Gītā*, III.3, Lord Kṛṣṇa also says: "O spotless one! it has been before declared by Me that the pursuit of men in this world is twofold: that of the thinkers, by the path of knowledge; that of the workers, by the path of action." These then are the two time-honoured paths of salvation, namely, action and knowledge. It will be observed, however, that action or intentional employment of will and energy may take two entirely distinct courses: the one manifesting itself in the performance of various sacrifices, penances, rituals, and other ceremonies prescribed in the sacred books or sanctioned by usage, in the hope of attaining particular results or rewards and deriving spiritual benefit therefrom; the other, taking a fundamentally opposite direction, abandons all hope of ever obtaining everything desired in this way, and gathering together all diffused energy and attention from the field of the world, turns inward upon the spiritual principle itself and proceeding upon the maxim of "endure and abstain", seeks, by the purification of body and mind, and by regulating and restraining their random workings, to bring into active play the latent powers of the soul which will then surmount all obstacles, conquering and carrying everything before it. Action in the latter form is called by the well-known name of yoga or Concentration or Communion.

Thus, therefore, we find—

i. The votary of knowledge who aims at keeping himself at a safe distance from the reach of human suffering by killing all desires in the mind, remaining for ever absorbed in the charming pursuit of understanding, more and more, in an endless manner, the nature of God and creation, and who from his empyrean altitude looks down, as it were, upon the things of the world;

ii. The man who strives to spread his kingdom over the universe, and takes recourse to particular practices for the realization of desired objects, thinking thereby to satisfy all his wants and thus indirectly to ensure unbroken happiness for himself here as well as in the world beyond;

iii. The *yogī* who stoutly turns away from the attraction of the world and concentrates his attention and energy all upon himself, so that the dormant possibilities of his divine nature may have unobstructed play and unbounded scope, in other words, that he may acquire 'powers' which will make everything possible for him; and

iv. The *bhakta*, or the votary of love, whose starting point is God Himself and who abnegates himself in His presence and who seeks not the indifference of the wise, the rewards of action, or the 'powers' of concentration, but whose only care in life is to serve the will of the Lord.

Now, this path of devotion, Nārada goes on to say, is higher than the three other ways of pious living as described above.

सो तु कर्म्मज्ञानयोगेभ्योप्याधिकतरा ।। २५ ।।

सा (*sā*), it, devotion. तु (*tu*), again. कर्म्मज्ञानयोगेभ्यः (*karma-jñāna-yogebhyaḥ*) than action, knowledge, and concentration. अपि (*api*), even. अधिकतरा (*adhikatarā*), higher.

25. It is, again higher than action, knowledge, and concentration.

Cf. *Gītā*, VI.46-47, where Lord Kṛṣṇa says: "The *yogī** is considered to be greater than the ascetic, greater also than the man of contemplation. The *yogī* is also greater than the man of action. Therefore, Arjuna, become a *yogī*. And of all the *yogins*, he who faithfully worships Me, with the inner self directed towards Me, is, in my opinion, the most concentrated." Śaṅkara also has said, मोक्षसाधनसामभ्याः भक्तिरेव गरीयसी, It is Devotion which is the greatest of all the means of Release.

फलरूपत्वात् ।। २६ ।।

फलरूपत्वात् (*phala-rūpatvāt*), from its re-appearance as its result.

26. (Devotion is higher than the others), because it is its own reward (whereas the followers of the other paths have ulterior objects in view, which necessarily divide them from God, and are, after all, finite in their nature, and hence fail to secure abiding peace for the soul).

ईश्वरस्याप्यभिमानिद्वेषित्वाद्दैन्यप्रियत्वाच्च ।। २७ ।।

ईश्वरस्य (*īśvarasya*), God's. अपि (*api*), also. अभिमानिद्वेषित्वात् (*abhimānī-dveṣitvāt*), from aversion to egotists. Note that it is not a positive feeling of disfavour on the part of God, but follows necessarily from the nature

*The *yogī* is one who enters into a living communion with God and perfectly realizes His immanence and activity everywhere in the world.

of things. For, in *Gītā*, IX.29, Lord Kṛṣṇa says: "I am equal to all created beings. There is no object of my particular favour or disfavour." And in commenting upon this, Nīlakaṇṭha writes: "As the fire, though it is devoid of attraction and other feelings, still removes the sensation of cold, only of those who are close by, and not of those who keep at a distance, so I, though equal to all, remove the bondage only of those who come to seek My refuge, and not of others. Therefore, aversion and attraction do not belong to Me." It follows, therefore, that egotism and other affections of the mind screen God from the view of men. दैन्यप्रियत्वात् (*dainya-priyatvāt*), Love of meekness. Cf. St. Matthew, V.3, 5: "Blessed (are) the poor in spirit; for theirs is the Kingdom of heaven." "Blessed (are) the meek; for they shall inherit the earth." Also St. Paul: "If any man thinketh that he is wise . . . let him become a fool that he may become wise." च (*ca*), and.

27. (Devotion is higher than the others), because of God's aversion to egotists and love of meekness.

The point is this—

The votary of love throws himself entirely at the mercy of God, while the rest strive to work out their salvation by themselves alone: some aspiring to knowledge, almost as extensive as God's, and, at the same time, killing all desire in their breasts; others attempting to extend their influence over the external word, thereby bringing all things within their easy reach; others, again, seeking to multiply their psychic powers which, they hope, will then satisfy all their desires no sooner than they arise. In the case of the devotee, his absolute dependence upon God brings him into daily and homely contact with the divine personality, whereas the others, running after their respective ambitions, are removed farther and farther away from Him.

Guru Nānaka reconciles the four Paths in a song in which he says—"Make *jñāna* your molasses, make *dhyāna* your *dhāwā* flowers, make *karma* your *kīkar* bark: mingle these in that distilling vessel—the world, and apply the plaster of *prema*. In this way the juice of *amṛta* will filter out. My son, he who with intoxicated mind drinks the juice of the Name tranquillity remains enraptured in the joy (of the Lord). In this song the reference is to the process practised in the days of the *guru* of distilling intoxicating liquor from molasses, *dhāwā* flowers and the bark of the *kīkar* tree, mixed together in a vessel the lid of which was generally plastered over."

तस्यो ज्ञानमेव साधनमित्येके ।। २८ ।।

ज्ञानम् (*jñānam*), knowledge. एव (*eva*), alone. तस्या (*tasyā*), its. Of devotion. साधनम् (*sādhanam*), source. इति (*iti*), thus. एके (*eke*), some.

28. Some say, knowledge is the source of devotion.

अन्योन्याश्रयत्वमित्येके ।। २९ ।।

अन्योन्याश्रयत्वम् (*anyonya-āśrayatvam*), mutual dependence (of knowledge and devotion). इति (*iti*), so. एके (eke), others.

29. Others declare their mutual dependence.

स्वयं फलरूपतेति ब्रह्मकुमारः ।। ३० ।।

स्वयं (*svayaṃ*), of itself. फलरूपता (*phala-rūpatā*), re-appearance as result or reward. इति (*iti*), so. ब्रह्मकुमारः (*brahma-kumāraḥ*), son of Brahmā; Nārada.

30. The son of Brahmā observes the resulting devotion as the fruit of itself.

राजगृहभोजनादिषु तथैव दृष्टत्वात् ।। ३१ ।।

राजगृहभोजनादिषु (*rāja-gṛha-bhojana-ādiṣu*), in the matter of feeding: (bestowing favours), in the royal household. तथा (*tathā*), the same. एव (*eva*), and nothing else. दृष्टत्वात् (*dṛṣṭatvāt*), having been witnessed.

31. (What has been said above holds good), the same, and nothing else, have been witnessed in the matter of feeding, bestowing favours, etc., in the royal household.

The metaphor may be explained at some length. The State is the household of the king. The members of that household may be roughly divided into four classes, viz., the wise men and the legislators, the civil and military administrators and keepers of internal and external peace, the chamberlain and his staff, and the waiters, beggars, and followers in general. Now, these four sets of people view the royal person from four distinct standpoints. Thus, the first cannot but recognise the fact that they are not, at least, inferior to the king in political wisdom and capacity for government, and may imagine that in each particular case ascension to the throne is a bare accident. Their attitude, therefore, is likely to become at times haughty and full of rivalry; at any rate, it is not always one of modesty and meekness. The second, again, are aware that actual administration of the affairs of the State is well-nigh impossible without their active co-operation, and that it is they who practically govern the kingdom. The keepers of the inner apartments also cannot fail to realize their unique position behind the curtain, and therefore they claim a certain amount of power over the king, because they have his secrets and his honour in their custody. In these circumstances, whatever they receive from the king, in the shape of salaries, rewards and remunerations, they accept the same as lawful demands by them on account of the service they render to the king, and not as loving presents from him. Pride and egotism are the principal traits in their character and conduct. The fourth class of absolute dependants, however, have not the lofty ambition which the wise men have of sailing alongside of the king, nor the sense of personal worth and importance of which the actual administrators are so keen aware, nor again the idea of power or influence over the king so naively claimed by the managers of the inner household. On the contrary, they sincerely recognise their insignificance and utterly helpless condition, and thereupon throw themselves entirely at the mercy of the king whom they regard as a loving father bestowing favours upon his children according to their fitness.

These four classes of subordinate human beings may be broadly likened to the votaries of knowledge, action, concentration, and devotion, respectivelly. And as they sow, so they reap. The well of the king's loving kindness, as of God, flows richly and freely towards his humble and wholehearted dependants; while the rest, from their egotism, sense of personal worth, and idea of power are more and more entangled in the meshes which they weave for themselves by their knowledge, action, and unique position; and consequently their vision becomes day by day circumscribed with regard to him in whose service they do after all live, move and have their being.

न तेन राजपरितोषः क्षुच्छान्तिर्वा ।। ३२ ।।

तेन (*tena*), for this. Because the followers of the other paths have their minds overshadowed with egotism and other affections. राजपरितोषः (*rāja-paritoṣaḥ*), King's pleasure. क्षुच्छान्तिः (*kṣut-śāntiḥ*), satisfaction of hunger. Hunger is here symbolical of desire in general. वा (*vā*), or. न (*na*), not.

32. For this neither the king finds any pleasure, nor the recipients any satisfaction of their desires (in the matter of distribution of royal favours).

Similarly, knowledge and action can neither move God favourably nor permanently satisfy desires.

तस्मात् सैव ग्राह्या मुमुक्षुभिः ।। ३३ ।।

तस्मात् (*tasmāt*), therefore. Since devotion is higher than the other paths. सा (*sā*), devotion. एव (*eva*), to the exclusion of the others. मुमुक्षुभिः (*mumukṣubhiḥ*), by those who desire salvation. ग्राह्या (*grāhyā*), worthy of being adopted.

33. Therefore, the path of devotion should be adopted, to the exclusion of the others, by those who desire salvation.

तस्याः साधनानि गायन्त्याचार्याः ।। ३४ ।।

आचार्य्याः (*acāryyāḥ*), masters. तस्याः (*tasyāḥ*), its; of devotion. साधनानि (*sādhanāni*), means. गायन्ति (*gāyanti*), recite.

34. The masters recite (as follows) the means (for the culture) of devotion.

Note: In the *Adhyātma Rāmāyaṇam*, III.10.22-30, we find:

(Addressing Śavarī, Rāma says): "Here (in the culture of devotion) the first means is, it has been taught, the company of the good; the second is conversation about My achievements; the third is recital of my virtues; the fourth means will be the occupation of expounding my words; the fifth is, O gentle one, constant and sincere worship of the preceptor, thinking that I am he; the sixth means has been said to be virtuousness, self-restraint, observance, etc., and ever-living attachment to My worship; the seventh is said to be religious service with every detail, reciting the *mantra* specially applicable to Me; greater adoration paid to My votaries, consciousness of Me in all beings, indifference to external objects, together with internal peace make up the eighth; and O lady, the ninth is the consideration of My essence. O auspicious one, devotion in the form of Love is produced in any and every one who employs this means in the shape of the ninefold (secondary or instrumental) devotion, no matter whether one be a woman or a man or belonging to the inferior creation. And as soon as devotional love is produced, one feels My essence, as it were, and one who becomes accomplished by the awareness of Me, attains liberation even in that birth. Therefore it is sure that devotion is the Source of Salvation."

Note: In aphorisms 26 and 30, it has been declared that devotion is its own means. It is not however suggested thereby that he who has no glow of devotion in him to begin with, can never hope to enter into a life devoted to the Lord, and consequently can never hope to attain salvation. Far from it; the doctrine of devotion is not a gospel of despair. It recognises and upholds that there is a regular course of training for the cultivation of devotion. It then sets forth the conditions under which the spark of devotion may gradually come to illuminate the entire inner and outer life of an ordinary mortal.

Hence—

तत्तु विषयत्यगात् सङ्गत्यागाच्च ।। ३५ ।।

तत् (*tat*), that; love of God. तु (*tu*), but. विषयत्यागात् (*viṣaya-tyāgāt*), from abandonment of sensible objects. सङ्गत्यागात् (*saṅga-tyāgāt*), from abandonment of attachment. च (*ca*), and.

35. But love of God is possible on the abandonment of all sensible objects and of every attachment to them.

अव्यावृत्तभजनात् ।। ३६ ।।

अव्यावृत्तभंजनात् (*a-vyāvṛtta-bhajanāt*), from unretarded practice; from cultivation without remiss.

36. (That arises also) from its cultivation without remiss, or from unflinching adoration of God.

Some take the *sūtram* as explaining the foregoing one. There the teaching is that love of God may be developed by turning away from the objects of desire. But how can one overcome their attraction? The reply is, they say, given in this *sūtram*, the meaning being: And the temptation of worldly desires may be overcome by sticking to the worship of God.

लोकेऽपि भगवद्गुणश्रवण कीर्त्तनात् ।। ३७ ।।

लोके (*loke*), in society. अपि (*api*), also. भगवद्गुणश्रवण कीर्त्तनात् (*bhagavad-guṇa-śravaṇa-kīrttanāt*), from listening to and singing of the virtues and attributes of the Great God.

37. (That springs also) from listening to and singing of the virtues and attributes of the Great God in society.

Cf. "I do not dwell in *vaikuṇṭha* (the highest heaven, the abode of Viṣṇu), nor in the hearts of *yogins*. O Nārada, I dwell there where my devotees sing."

Note: This *sūtram* has been otherwise explained thus: "In this world there are found instances which show that love of God may be cultivated by listening to and singing of the attributes of God."

Cf. The saying of Zu'n-nūn the Egyptian: "Music is a divine influence which stirs the heart to seek God: those who listen to it spiritually attain unto God, and those who listen to it sensually fall into unbelief." About mystic dance it has been said: "When the heart throbs and rapture grows intense, and the agitation of ecstasy is manifested, and conventional forms are gone, this is not dancing nor bodily indulgence, but a dissolution of the soul."

मुख्यतस्तु महत्कृपयैव भगवद्कृपालेशाद्वा ।। ३८ ।।

मुख्यत: (*mukhyataḥ*), principally. तु (*tu*), but. महत्कृपया (*mahat-kṛpayā*) by the grace of the great ones. एव (*eva*), surely. वा (*vā*), or, in other words. There obtains a community of selves between the great ones and their Great God. And when these great ones are moved by compassion towards their mortal brothers, it is their Great God who works in them. भगवद्कृपालेशात् (*bhagavad-kṛpā-leśāt*), from the touch of divine compassion. That is why St. Clement of Alexandria said: "Man predestines God as much as God predestines man"—for, as Bossnet explains: "The soul gives itself as the spouse to her lover: It gives itself to God as actively and freely as God gives himself to it. For God raises its power of free election to its highest pitch on account of the desire He has to be chosen freely." "See also *Quran,* XXIX.69. "Whosoever shall strive for Our sake, We shall guide him into Our ways."

38. But that is obtained, principally and surely, by the race of the great ones, or in other words, from the touch of divine compassion.

"This Self cannot be realized by discourse, nor by intelligence, nor by deep learning. It can be realized by him only whom it favours: him this Self favours with its manifestation." (*Muṇḍaka Upaniṣad,* III.ii.3)

The beneficial influence of good company has been described in *Śrīmadbhāgavatam,* III.25.25, in these words:

"In the company of the great prevail talks which perfectly convey My majesty and which soothe the heart and the ear. From listening to these, faith, attachment, and devotion will succeed one another towards Him who is the way to salvation."

Note: In some editions this *sūtram* has been split into two, viz., "Principally, however, through the kindness of the great", and "And also by the mercy of God."

महत्सङ्गस्तु दुर्लभोऽगम्योऽमोघश्च ।। ३६ ।।

महत्सङ्ग: (*mahat-saṅgaḥ*), companionship of the great. तु (*tu*), again, but. दुर्लभ: (*durlabhaḥ*), difficult of attainment. अगम्य: (*agamyaḥ*), unapprochable; inscrutable; of unassignable cause. अमोघः (*amoghaḥ*), infallible. च (*ca*), and.

39. Companionship of the great is, again, difficult of attainment. It is hardly possible to assign how and when men may be taken into the society of the great. But once obtained, association with the great ones is infallible in its operation.

लभ्यतेऽपि तत्कृपयैव ।। ४० ।।

तत्कृपया (*tat-kṛpayā*), by His (i.e., God's) grace. एव (*eva*), only. लभ्यते (*labhyate*), is obtained gained. अपि (*api*), and.

40. And companionship of the great is gained by the grace of God alone.

But how can the grace of God be followed by the response of the good? The sequence does not appear to be necessary. Not so; for, God and His good men are but one being, so to say. This is the text of the following *sūtram.*

तस्मिंस्तज्जने भेदाभावात् ।। ४१ ।।

तस्मिन् (*tasmin*), in Him. तज्जने (*tat-jane*), in His man. भेदाभावात् (*bheda-abhāvāt*), because there is no distinction.

41. Because there is no distinction between Him and His man.

St. Paul says: "He that is joined with the Lord is one spirit" (I. Cor. VI. 18). Cf. also the saying of Zu'n-nūn of Egypt: "They move as God causes them to move and their words are the words of God, which roll upon their tongues, and their sight is the sight of God, which has entered their eyes."

Man *is* what he loves, said St. Augustine.

Jalāl-ud-dīn Rūmī, says:

"The motion of every atom is towards its origin;
A man comes to be the thing on which he is bent.
By the attraction of fondness and yearning, the soul and the heart
Assume the qualities of the Beloved, who is the Soul of souls."

In another ode he says:

"O my soul, I searched from end to end: I saw in thee naught save the Beloved;
Call me not infidel, O my soul, if I say that thou thyself art He."

And yet more plainly:

"Ye who in search of God, of God, pursue.
Ye need not search for God is you, is you!
Why seek ye something that was missing ne'er!
Save you none is, but you are—where, oh, where?"

तदेव साध्यतां तदेव साध्यताम् ।। ४२ ।।

तत् (*tat*), that; love of God. एव (*eva*), alone. साध्यताम् (*sādhyatām*), should be cultivated, practised, striven after.

42. Strive after love of God alone, strive after love of God alone.

दुःसङ्ग सर्व्वथैव त्याज्यः ।। ४३ ।।

दुःसङ्गः (*duḥ-saṅgaḥ*), evil company. सर्व्वथा (*sarvvathā*), by all means. त्याज्यः (*tyājyaḥ*), to be given up. एव (*eva*), certainly.

43. Evil company should be certainly shunned by all means.

कामक्रोधमोहस्मृतिभ्रंशबुद्धिनाशसर्वनाशकारणत्वात् ।। ४४ ।।

काम (*kāma*), desire, lust. क्रोध (*krodha*), anger, wrath. मोह (*moha*), bewilderment, infatuation. स्मृतिभ्रंश (*smṛti-bhraṃśa*), lapse of memory. बुद्धिनाश (*buddhi-nāśa*), loss of understanding or perception of truth. सर्वनाश (*sarva-nāśa*), total ruin. कारणत्वात् (*kāraṇatvāt*), being the cause of.

44. Because it is the cause of lust, resentment, bewilderment, lapse of memory, loss of understanding, and total ruin (of piety and liberation).

Cf. Tulsīdāsa—"Rāma and Kāma cannot go hand in hand."

In this connection compare also *Gītā,* II.62-63, "Attachment grows in the man towards objects which bind down, while he turns them round and round in his own mind. Attachment begets lust, and lust, resentment. Resentment gives rise to bewilderment, and bewilderment, to lapse of memory. Lapse of memory leads to loss of understanding, and from loss of understanding he is finally lost."

तरङ्गायिता अपीमे सङ्गात् समुद्रायन्ति ।। ४५ ।।

तरङ्गायिताः (*taraṅgāyitāḥ*), playing in ripples. अपि (*api*), even. इमे (*ime*), these; lust, etc. सङ्गात् (*saṅgāt*), in cooperation with evil association. समुद्रायन्ति (*samudrāyanti*), behave like the sea.

45. These evil tendencies, playing even in ripples from nature, ultimately behave as the stormy sea in cooperation with evil association.

कस्तरति कस्तरति मायां? यः सङ्गं त्यजति यो महानुभावं सेवते निर्म्ममो भवति।।४६।।

कः (*kaḥ*), who (interrogative). मायां (*māyām*), that which conditions the primal unconditioned; condition; determination; negation; limitation. The translation of माया as 'illusion', in the first instance, is not satisfactory. It is also misleading. Cf. Spinoza: *Omnes determinatio negatio est*—all determination is negation. तरति (*tarati*), crosses over. यः (*yaḥ*), who (relative). सङ्गं (*saṅgaṃ*), evil association, attachment to objects. त्यजति (*tyajati*), gives up. महानुभावं (*mahā-anubhāvaṃ*), a large-hearted man; great men. सेवते (*sevate*), keeps by. निर्ममः (*nirmamaḥ*), void of 'myness', selfless. भवति (*bhavati*), becomes.

46. Who overcomes all limitation? Who overcomes? He who holds aloof from unholy association, keeps company with men of large hearts, and becomes selfless.

यो विविक्तस्थानं सेवते यो लोकबन्धमुन्मूलयति निस्त्रैगुणयो भवति यो योगक्षेमं त्यजति।।४७।।

यः (*yaḥ*), who विविक्तस्थानं (*vivikta-sthānaṃ*), holy or lonely spot. सेवते (*sevate*), resorts to. लोकबन्धं (*loka-bandham*), worldly desires or bonds. उन्मूलयति (*unmūlayati*), roots out. निस्त्रैगुण्यः (*nistraiguṇyaḥ*), unworldly, the world of desires being the composition of the well-known principles of illumination, evolution, and involution. The three *guṇas* are "aspects of one and the same thing, viz., *prakṛti* and are reproduced in every phenomenon". "Cosmically and individually *sattva* is the factor of freedom, insight and bliss, *rajas* of energy, *tamas* of passivity. Passivity results in cosmic stability and individual inertia; *rajas* in cosmic activity and individual passion; *sattva* in cosmic obedience to law and individual progress by means of such obedience." ("Zero"). भवति (*bhavati*), is. योगक्षेमम् (*yoga-kṣemaṃ*), acquisition and preservation. त्यजति (*tyajati*), forsakes.

47. Who retires to a holy, lonely spot, who roots out worldly bonds, who is unworldly, and who forsakes both acquisition and preservation of desirables.

Cf. *Gītā*, II.45 where Lord Kṛṣṇa says: "The Vedas (in their ritual portions) have the world for their object. O Arjuna! Become unworldly, uninfluenced by contraries or duals, always fixed in the principle of illumination, unmindful of aquisition and preservation, and self-controlled.

यः कर्म्मफलं त्यजति कर्म्मणि संन्यस्यति ततो निर्द्वन्द्वो भवति।। ४८।।

यः (*yaḥ*), who. कर्म्मफलं (*karmma-phalaṃ*), the fruits of actions. त्यजति (*tyajati*), gives up. Has no eye to. कर्म्माणि (*karmāṇi*), actions. संन्यस्यति (*saṃnyasyati*) dedicates to God. ततः (*tataḥ*), then. Thereby. निर्द्वन्द्वः (*nirdvandvaḥ*), free from the influence of contraries, such as pleasure and pain, good and bad, hot and cold. भवति (*bhavati*), becomes.

48. Who has no eye to the fruits of his actions, who dedicates all actions to God or who in everything does the will of God, and thereby becomes free from the influence of all contraries.

यो वेदानपि संन्यस्यति केवलमविच्छिन्नानुरागंलभते।। ४६।।

यः (*yaḥ*), who. वेदान् (*vedān*), the sacred books. अपि (*api*), even. संन्यस्यति (*saṃnyasyati*), lays aside. केवलं (*kevalaṃ*), undivided. अविच्छिन्नानुरागं (*avicchinna anurāgaṃ*), uninterrupted flow of affection or love. लभते (*labhate*), attains, develops.

49. Who lays aside even the sacred writings and who develops an undivided and uninterrupted flow of love towards God.

Says St. John of the Cross, "All the images of the imagination are confined within very narrow limits, and the Divine Wisdom, to which the understanding ought to unite itself, is infinite, absolutely pure and aboslutely simple, and it is not confined within the limits of any distinct, particular or finite mind. The soul which desires to unite itself to the Divine Wisdom must necessarily bear some proportion and likeness to it, and consequently it must shake itself free from the images of the imagination which would give it limits. It must not attach itself to any particular form of thought, but must be pure, simple, without limits or material ideas, in order to approach in some degree to God, who cannot be expressed by any bodily likeness, or by any single finite conception."

सः तरति सः तरति लोकांस्तारयति।। ५०।।

सः (*saḥ*), he. तरति (*tarati*), overcomes. लोकान् (*lokān*), mankind. तारयति (*tārayati*), helps to overcome.

50. He overcomes all limitation, he overcomes all limitation; he helps mankind to overcome their limitations.

Some readers distinguish between the first and the second 'he'. They say that men come to love God either by instinct or by education, and that the previous aphorisms have reference to the latter only. Now, if these men overcome limitation, it goes without saying that instinctive lovers of God also do so. Therefore, the second they refers to them, as also the last sentence. The *sūtram*, therefore, according to them, means—"He overcomes limitation. The instinctive lover of God also overcomes limitation. And not only so, but he also helps others to overcome their limitation."

अनिर्वचनीयं प्रेमस्वरूपम् ।। ५१ ।।

प्रेमस्वरूपं (*prema-svarūpaṃ*), the nature of love towards God. (Vide *supra*, p.xxii.) अनिर्वचनीयं (*anirvacanīyaṃ*), not capable of being expressed in words.

51. The nature of love towards God is not capable of being described in words.

The *Śrīmadbhāgavatam*, in III.25.32, has roundly described it thus—

"Devotion to God is the motiveless and spontaneous function in the divine form of Illumination, of the shining senses which mark out objects, or of their presiding principles, belonging to a man whose mind has become steady by the performance of scriptural rites."

"Gnostics", says Ibn-al-'Arabī, the great Arab mystic, "cannot impart their feelings to other men; they can only indicate them symbolically to those who have begun to experience the like."

मूकास्वादनवत् ।। ५२ ।।

मूकास्वादनवत् (*mūka-āsvādana-vat*), like the taste of a dumb person.

52. (The nature of love is as indescribable) as the taste of a dumb person.

"Gnosis", says a mystic of Islam, "is nearer to silence than to speech." What then association with the great and good will avail, if the enthusiasm of devotion is untranslatable in words and consequently incommunicable from person to person? To this the reply is that the operation of devotion is telepathic and not through any grosser medium.

"Love is not be learned from men: it is one of God's gifts and comes of His grace." Hence—

प्रकाश्यते क्वापि पात्रे ।। ५३ ।।

क्व अपि (*kva api*), some; where everything is favourable to its appearance; fit. पात्रे (*pātre*), receptable. प्रकाश्यते (*prakāśyate*), is revealed.

Cf. " 'Tis the sun's self that lets the sun be seen."

"Man's love of God", says Hujwīrī, an Islamic mystic, "is a quality which manifests itself, in the heart of the pious believer, in the form of veneration and magnification, so that he seeks to satisfy the Beloved and becomes imaptient and restless in his desire for vision of Him, and cannot rest with any one except Him, and grows familiar with the recollection of Him, and abjures the recollection of everything besides." "I fancied that I loved Him", said Bāyazīd, another mystic, "but on consideration I saw that His love preceded mine."

गुणरहितं कामनारहितं प्रतिक्षणवर्द्धमानमविच्छिन्नं सूक्ष्मतरमनुभवरूपम् ।। ५४ ।।

गुणरहितं (*guṇa-rahitaṃ*), devoid of qualification. कामनारहितं (*kāmanā-rahitaṃ*), bereft of desire. प्रतिक्षणवर्द्धमानं (*pratikṣaṇa-vardhamānaṃ*), accumulating at every moment. अविच्छिन्नं (*avicchinnaṃ*), of ceaseless flow. सूक्ष्मतरं (*sūkṣmataraṃ*), subtler. अनुभवरूपं (*anubhava-rūpaṃ*), of the form of feeling.

54. Devoid of qualification, bereft of desire, growing in volume and intensity at every moment, and having a ceaseless flow, it is of the form of subtler feeling.

तत् प्राप्य तदेवावलोकयति तदेव शृणोति तदेव चिन्तयति ।। ५५ ।।

तत् (*tat*), that Love, Devotion. प्राप्य (*prāpya*), having obtained. तत् (*tat*), that. The object of love. एव (*eva*), alone अवलोकयति (*avalokayati*), looks upon. शृणोति (*śṛṇoti*), hears about. चिन्तयति (*caintayati*), thinks of.

55. Having once obtained that, (the devotee) looks only upon the object of his devotion, entertains talks only about Him, and thinks nobly of Him.

But how does this happen? Well, men first love God with an object. Then, in the nature of things, by a transference of interest, they love God without any object, for love sake, or, what is the same thing, for the sake of God Who is love. In the next aphorism, therefore, we have a classification of those men who wait upon God with an ulterior end in view.

गौणी त्रिधा गुणभेदादार्त्तादिभेदाद्वा ।। ५६ ।।

गौणी (*gauṇī*), secondary. Derivative. Desire-born. Indirect. गुणभेदात् (*guṇa-bhedāt*), according to the difference of the principles viz., of illumination, evolution, and involution. वा (*vā*), or, in other words. आर्त्तादिभेदात् (*ārtta-ādi-bhedāt*), according to the distinction of the worshippers as the afflicted, the inquisitive, and the entreative or needful. त्रिधा (*tridhā*), threefold.

56. Devotion which is born of desire, becomes threefold, according as the one or other of the principles of illumination, evolution,

and involution dominates the conduct of the devotee, or, in other words, according as the worshippers fall into the three classes of the afflicted, the inquisitive, and entreative.

In *Gītā*, VII.16 and 19, it has been said that four sets of fortunate men wait upon God, viz., the afflicted, the inquisitive, the entreative, and the wise of high soul with whom God is the be-all and end-all of life. Of this last class Nārada speaks as the immediate devotees of God in aphorism 67.

उत्तरस्मादुत्तरस्मात् पूर्वपूर्वा श्रेयाय भवति ।। ५७ ।।

उत्तरस्मादुत्तरस्मात् (*uttarasmād-uttarasmāt*), than each succeeding one. पूर्वपूर्वा (*pūrva-pūrvā*), each preceding one. श्रेयाय (*śreyāya*), for the better. भवति (*bhavati*), is, works.

57. If each preceding kind of devotion works for the higher good than each succeeding one.

अन्यस्मात् सौलभ्यं भक्तौ ।। ५८ ।।

भक्तौ (*bhaktau*), in devotion. अन्यस्मात् (*anyasmāt*), than any other. सौलभ्यं (*saulabhyaṃ*), cheapness. The nature of being easily obtained.

58. In devotion (the fulfilment of the desire to enter into intimate fellowship with God or attainment of salvation, is) easier than in any thing else.

The path of devotion is easier than that of either knowledge, or action, or concentration. Because—

i. Action and concentration do not directly lead to salvation but only help on the progress of knowledge and devotion.

ii. Again, they are beset with difficulties and dangers of their own, as the followers of them gradually come to acquire 'powers' which are often liable to abuse.

iii. Indifference to worldly desire is a condition precedent to the employment of knowledge. So is also the arrest of all worldly activity. But one may safely and successfully pursue the path of devotion, provided only that one believes in the existence, nature, and attributes of God, and dedicates the fruits of one's action to Him, in other words, does the will of God in everything.

iv. Again, the pursuit of knowledge is dry and not very interesting in itself, while that of devotion is sweet and enjoyable.

But, it may be asked, how do you prove this? We reply that it does not at all stand in need of any proof. Hence—

प्रमाणान्तरस्यानपेक्षत्वात् स्वयं प्रमाणात्वात् ।। ५६ ।।

प्रमाणान्तरस्य (*pramāṇa-antarasya*), of other proof. अनपेक्षत्वात् (*ana-pekṣatvāt*), because of the absence of the need. स्वयं (*svayaṃ*), itself. प्रमाणत्वात् (*pramāṇatvāt*), being evidence.

59. Because there is no need of any other demonstration, since it is proof of itself.

शान्तिरूपात् परमानन्दरूपाच्च ।। ६० ।।

शान्तिरूपात् (*śānti-rūpāt*), because it transforms itself into the state of internal peace. परमानन्दरूपात् (*paramānanda-rūpāt*), because it takes the form of high ecstasy. च (*ca*), and.

60. The path of devotion is easy, because it fills the mind of the devotee with peace and high ecstasy.

The devotee then forgets everything, even himself. He truly lives only for God, nay, he lives in God. But, then a very practical question arises: What with the world? To this it is said, in the next aphorism, that life in God can on no occasion seriously interfere with life on earth, and that, therefore, no anxiety should be entertained on this score regarding the conduct of social life. Thus—

लोकहानौ चिन्ता न कार्य्या निवेदितात्मलोकवेदत्वात् ।। ६१ ।।

लोकहानौ (*loka-hānau*), in respect of social disorganisation. चिन्ता (*cintā*), thought, anxiety. न (*na*), not. कार्य्या (*kāryā*), should be cherished. निवेदितात्म-लोकवेदत्वात् (*nivedita-ātma-loka-vedatvāt*), because of the fact that the self, and social and scriptural morality have been dedicated to God.

61. No anxious thought need be entertained in respect of social disorganisation, seeing that the devotee has consecrated his self and customary and scriptural morality all to the Lord.

Should then customary rules of conduct be disregarded altogether? By no means. For—

न तत्सिद्धौ लोकव्यवहारो हेयः किन्तु फलत्यागस्तत्साधनञ्च कार्यमेव ।। ६२ ।।

तत्सिद्धौ (*tat-siddhau*), in the development of devotion. लोकव्यवहारः (*loka-vyavahāraḥ*), social custom and usage. न (*na*), not. हेयः (*heyaḥ*), to be neglected किन्तु (*kintu*), but. फलत्यागः (*phala-tyāgaḥ*), surrender of consequences, तत्साधनं (*tatsādhanaṃ*), its performance. च (*ca*), and, meaning 'at the same time', together with. कार्यं (*kāryaṃ*), should be attended to. एव (*eva*), certainly.

62. In the development of devotion, one must not neglect to observe social customs and ceremonies, but, on the contrary, one should surely attend to their due performance together with the surrender of all consequences to God.

"Although sacrifices and the like are enjoined with a view to the origination of knowledge (in accordance with the passage 'They desire to know', *Bṛ. Up.,* IV.4.22), it is only knowledge in the form of meditation which—being daily practised, constantly improved by repetition and continued up to death—is the means of reaching Brahman, and hence all the works connected with the different conditions of life are to be performed throughout life only for the purpose of originating such knowledge. This the Sūtrakāra declares in *Ved. Sū.*, III.4.33; IV.1.12, 16, and other places." (Thibaut's translation, *SBE*, vol. XLVIII, p. 16.)

स्त्रीधननास्तिकचरित्रं न श्रवणीयम् ।। ६३ ।।

स्त्रीधननास्तिकचरित्रं (*strī-dhana-nāstika-caritraṃ*), woman, wealth, and the conduct of the unbelievers, i.e., those who deny the authority of the Vedas and the existence of God. न (*na*), not. श्रवणीयम् (*sravaṇīyaṃ*), should be listened to.

63. The aspirant after devotion should not listen to talks about woman, wealth and the conduct of unbelievers.

In this and the following as well as in aphorisms 43-45, 73-74, the impediments to the cultivation of devotion have been enumerated.

अभिमानदम्भादिकं त्याज्यम् ।। ६४ ।।

अभिमानदम्भादिकं (*abhimāna-dambha-ādikaṃ*), egotism, or self-assertion, pride, etc. त्याज्यम् (*tyājyam*), should be forsaken.

64. Self-assertion, pride, etc. should be forsaken.

Now, it is almost next to impossible to abandon these natural tendencies of frail human nature by an effort, as it were. The proper remedy is to divert their courses. And where God becomes the object of such passions, they lose their wickedness and gradually put on a noble aspect. Therefore it is laid down in the next aphorism.

तदर्पिताखिलाचारः सन् कामक्रोधाभिमानादिकं तस्मिन्नेव करणीयम् ।। ६५ ।।

तदर्पिताखिलाचारः (*tadarpita-akhila-ācāraḥ*), one who has devoted all one's conduct to him. सन् (*san*), being becoming. कामक्रोधाभिमानादिकं (*kāma-krodha-abhimāna-ādikaṃ*). Desire, resentment, self-assertion, etc. तस्मिन् (*tasmin*), in him. एव (*eva*), only. करणीयम् (*karaṇīyam*), should be done, or shown or cherished.

65. Having once devoted all his conduct to Him, he should show (if at all), desire, resentment, self-assertion, etc., only to Him.

त्रिरूपभङ्गपूर्वकं नित्यदास्यनित्यकान्ताभजनात्मकं प्रेम कार्यं प्रेमैव कार्यम् ।। ६६ ।।

त्रिरूपभङ्गपूर्वकं (*tri-rūpa-bhaṅga-pūrvakaṃ*), having broken through the three forms (see *sūtram* 56) of secondary devotion modified by the principles of illumination, evolution, and involution. नित्यदास्यनित्यकान्ता-भजनात्मकं (*nityadāsyanityakāntā-bhajana-ātmakaṃ*), having its principle in those stages in the development of devotion which are known as constant service as of a servant to his master and constant service as of a wife to her husband, the intermediate stages (see Ś. 82) being also included. These stages of devotion are not modified by the three principles प्रेम (*prema*), love. कार्यं (*kāryam*), should be cultivated. एव (*eva*), only.

66. Having kept clear of the three modified forms of secondary devotion, one should cultivate love and, love alone, which has its principle in those stages of devotion, which are known as constant service and constant wifely conduct.

भक्ता एकान्तिनो मुख्याः ।। ६७ ।।

एकान्तिनः (*ekāntinaḥ*), single-hearted. Those whose only object of love and devotion is God. भक्ताः (*bhaktāḥ*), devotees. मुख्याः (*mukhyāḥ*), principal, primary, direct, immediate.

67. The primary votaries are those who have one end only in view.

Cf. *Śrīmadbhāgavatam,* III.29, 13-14, where *Bhagavān* says—

"People do not accept fellowship in residence with Me, prosperity equal to Mine, nearness to Me, appearance in the same form as I appear, or even unification with Me, even when these are offered to them; they only pray for employment in My service. It is this link of devotion which has been said to be the absolute, by which overcoming attachment to the world, they become fit for attaining My nature."

कण्ठावरोधरोमाश्रुभिःपरस्परं लपमानाः पावयन्ति कुलानि पृथिवीञ्च ।। ६८ ।।

कण्ठावरोधरोमाश्रुभिः (*kaṇṭha-avarodha-roma-aśrubhiḥ*), (marked out) by choking voice, hairs standing on end, and tears. परस्परं (*parasparaṃ*), amongst themselves, with one another. लपमानः (*lapamānaḥ*), conversing. कुलानि (*kulāni*), families. पृथिवीं (*pṛthivīṃ*), the earth. च (*ca*), and.

पावयन्ति (*pāvayanti*), purify.

68. Conversing together with a choking voice, with hairs standing on end, and with tears flowing, they purify their families as well as the earth.

In *Gītā*, X.9, Lord Kṛṣṇa says, "Having their minds fixed upon Me and their life directed to Me, enlightening one another, and constantly talking about Me, My devotees become satisfied and delighted."

तीर्थीकुर्वन्ति तीर्थानि सुकर्म्मीकुर्वन्ति कर्म्माणि सच्छास्त्रीकुर्वन्ति शास्त्राणि ।। ६९ ।।

तीर्थानि (*tīrthāni*), places called by the name. Holy sites. तीर्थीकुर्वन्ति (*tīrthīkurvanti*), make holy places. कर्माणि (*karmāṇi*), actions. सुकर्मीकुर्वन्ति (*sukarmīkurvanti*), make meritorious actions. शास्त्राणि (*śāstrāṇi*), writings so-called, rules of conduct. सच्छास्त्रीकुर्वन्ति (*sat-śāstrīkurvanti*), make sacred scriptures.

69. They add holiness to holy sites, they give to actions the character of meritoriousness; they raise mere writings to the status of the sacred scriptures.

तन्मयाः ।। ७० ।।

तन्मयाः (*tan-mayāḥ*), full of that. Filled with the presence of God. Merged or absorbed in him. Cf. "The whole world is the manifestation of Viṣṇu."

70. In and around them, they realise the presence of God everywhere and at all times.

A familiar instance of such absolute identification is found in the popular notion that the body is the entire man,—the identification of the soul with the body.

"The Soul (when united to God)", says St. John of the Cross, "falls at first into a state of great forgetfulness. With regard to exterior things if then shows so great a negligence and so great a contempt of self that, lost it God, it forgets to eat or drink, and it no longer knows if it has done a thing or not, or whether or not it has been spoken to by any one. . . . But once the soul has become firmly established in the habit of a union, which is its sovereign good, it no longer forgets reasonable things, and things of moral and physical necessity. On the contrary, it is more perfect when engaged in works suitable to its state of life, although it accomplishes them by the help of images and knowledge which God excites in a special manner in the memory. All the powers of the soul are, as it were, transformed in God."

Spinoza also says: "Man advances in perfection in proportion to the perfection of that object which he loves above all other things, and which loves him in return."

मोदन्ते पितरो नृत्यन्ति देवताः सनाथा चेयं भूर्भवति।। ७१।।

पितरः (*pitaraḥ*), the departed ancestors, forefathers. मोदन्ते (*modante*), rejoice. देवताः (*devatāḥ*), the shining ones; the celestials. नृत्यन्ति (*nṛtyanti*), dance. इयं (*iyaṃ*), this. भूः (*bhūḥ*), earth. च (*ca*), and. सनाथा (*sanāthā*), provided with a lord; secure. भवति (*bhavati*), becomes.

71. (At their devotion) their forefathers rejoice, the celestials dance and this earth becomes secure as though in the guardianship of a lord.

नास्ति तेषु जातिविद्यारूपकुलधनक्रियादिभेदः।। ७२।।

तेषु (*teṣu*), amongst them, within their rank. जातिविद्यारूपकुलधनक्रियादिभेदः (*jāti-vidyā-rūpa-kula-dhana-kriyā-ādi-bhedaḥ*), distinctions of birth, learning, appearance, family, wealth, observance, etc. न (*na*), not. अस्ति (*asti*), exists.

72. Amongst them there exist no distinctions of birth, learning, appearance, family, wealth, observance, and the like.

In the *Adhyātma Rāmāyaṇam,* III.10, 20, Rāma says, "Sex, birth, reputation, status, etc., do not confer any title to my worship; only devotion (*adhikāra,* or fitness, competence, according to a different reading) does." Cf. Guru Nānaka—"He alone is low-caste who forgets the lord." As regards learning, "Piety without Science", says St. Theresa, "may fill souls with illusions and inspire them with a taste for childish and silly devotions", and further "I have found that, provided they are men of good morals, they are better with no learning at all than with only a little, for in the former case, at least, they do not trust to their own lights but take counsel of really enlightened persons."

यतस्तदीयाः।। ७३।।

यतः (*yataḥ*), since तदीयाः (*tadīyāḥ*), belonging to him, his.

78. Since they all belong to Him.

वादो नवालम्ब्यः।। ७४।।

वादः (*vādaḥ*), Vain discussion. न (*na*), not. अवलम्ब्यः (*avalambyaḥ*), should be undertaken.

74. Vain discussion should not be undertaken (by those who aspire

to devotion, regarding the existence or attributed of God).

It has been pointed out in the *Kaṭhopaniṣad*—

"How else can that be conceived except that it exists?"

बाहुल्यावकाशत्वादिनयतत्वाच्च।। ७५।।

बाहुल्यावकाशत्वात् (*bāhulya-avakāśatvāt*), because of room or occasion for futility. अनियतत्वात् (*aniyatatvāt*), on account of uncertainty, or *regressus ad infinitum.* च (*ca*), and.

75. (Vain discussion about God must not be encouraged) because it can go on indefinitely, and there will be still no certainty that it will ever arrive at the truth.

भक्तिशास्त्राणि मननीयानि तद्बोधकर्म्माणि करणीयानि।। ७६।।

भक्तिशास्त्राणि (*bhaktiśāstrāṇi*), treatises on devotion. There are quite a lot of them. The most important ones are: the *Gītā, Śrīmadbhāgavatam, Viṣṇupurāṇam, Adhyātma Rāmāyaṇam*, etc. मननीयानि (*mananīyāni*), should be thought over or reflected upon. तद्बोधकर्म्माणि (*tadbodha-karmmāṇi*), observances prescribed in them as binding. करणीयानि (*karaṇīyāni*), should be performed.

76. Treatises on devotion should be studied with attention and observances therein laid down as binding should be performed.

सुखदुःखेच्छालाभादित्यक्ते काले प्रतीक्षमाणे क्षणार्द्धमपि व्यर्थ न नेयम्।। ७७।।

सुखदुःखेच्छालाभादित्यक्ते (*sukha-duḥkha-icchā-lābhādi-tyakte*), left out by pleasure, pain, desire, gain, etc. Cf. अनवकाशिनः, without leisure, in *Bhaktiratnāvalī*, I.9. Or it might be taken to mean, altogether unoccupied by pleasure, etc. काले (*kāle*), in time. प्रतीक्षमाणे (*pratīkṣamāṇe*), being looked up to. Being waited for. क्षणार्द्धं (*kṣaṇārddham*), half a moment. अपि (*api*), even. व्यर्थं (*vyartham*), in vain. न (*na*), not. नेयम् (*neyam*), should be passed.

77. Half a moment even should not be passed in vain, as all the time one has for divine contemplation is the little that remains after what is given to the thought and experience of pleasure, pain, desire, gain, and the rest.

अहिंसासत्यशौचदयास्तिक्यादिचारित्र्याणि परिपालनीयानि।। ७८।।

अहिंसासत्यशौचदयास्तिक्यादिचारित्र्याणि (*ahiṃsā-satya-śauca-dayā-āstikya-ādicāritryāṇi*), harmlessness, truthfulness, cleanliness, kindness, faith in God and revelation, and other excellence of character. परिपालनीयानि

(*paripālanīyāni*), should be strictly adopted.

78. They should carefully observe harmlessness, truthfulness, cleanliness of body and mind, kindness, faith in God and revelation, and other excellences of character.

Cf. *Śrībhāṣya* of Rāmānuja—

"The *vyākhyākāra* also declares that steady remembrance results only—from abstention, and so on; his words being 'This (viz., steady remembrance meditation) is obtained through abstention (*viveka*), freeness of mind (*vimoka*), repetition (*abhyāsa*), works (*kriyā*), virtuous conduct (*kalyāṇa*), freedom from dejection (*anavasāda*), absence of exultation (*anudharṣa*); according to feasibility and Scriptural statement. The *vyākhyākāra* also gives definitions of all these terms. Abstention (*viveka*) means keeping the body clean from all food, impure either owing to species (such as the flesh of certain animals), abode (such as food belonging to a Cāṇḍāla or the like) or accidental cause (such as food into which a hair or the like has fallen). The Scriptural passage authorising this point is *Ch. Up.*, VII.26, 'The food being pure, the mind becomes pure, the mind being pure, there results steady remembrance.' Freeness of mind (*vimoka*) means absence of attachment of desires. The authoritative passage here is 'Let him meditate with a calm mind' (*Ch. Up.*, III.14.1). Repetition means continued practice. For this point the *bhāṣyakāra* quotes an authoritative text from Smṛti, viz., 'Having constantly been absorbed in the thought of that being' (*sadā tadbhāvabhāvitaḥ, Bh. G.*, VIII.6). By works (*kriyā*) is understood the performance, according to one's ability, of the five great Sacrifices. The authoritative passages here are, 'This person who performs works is the best of those who know Brahman' (*Muṇḍ. Up.*, III.1.4), and 'Him Brāhmaṇas seek to know by recitation of the Veda, by sacrifice, by gifts, by penance, by fasting.' (*Bṛ. Up.*, IV.4.22). By virtuous conduct (*kalyāṇam*) are meant truthfulness, honesty, kindness, liberality, gentleness, absence of covetousness. Confirmatory texts are 'By truth he is to be obtained' (*Muṇḍ. Up.*, III.1.5), and 'to them belongs that pure Brahman world' (*Pr. Up.*, I.16). That lowness of spirit or want of cheerfulness which results from unfavourable conditions of place or time and the remembrance of causes of sorrow, is denoted by the term 'dejection', the contrary of this is freedom from dejection. The relevant scriptural passage is 'This self cannot be obtained by one lacking in strength' (*Muṇḍ. Up.*, III.2.4). 'Exultation' is that satisfaction of mind which springs from circumstances opposite to those just mentioned; the contrary is 'absence of exultation.' Overgreat satisfaction also stands in the way (of meditation). The scriptural passage for this is 'Calm, subdued, etc.' (*Bṛ. Up.,* IV.4.23). What the *vyākhyākāra* means to say is therefore that knowledge is realised only through the performances of the duly prescribed works, on the part of a person fulfilling all the enumerated conditions." (Thibaut's translation, *SBE,* vol. XLVIII, pp. 17-18.)

But the mind is ever unsteady. How then to steady it in God? The next two aphorisms teach us how to fix the mind in devotion to the Lord.

सर्वदा सर्वभावेन निश्चिन्तैर्भगवानेव भजनीयः ।। ७६ ।।

निश्चिन्तैः (*niścintaiḥ*), by those who have no scruple, no hestitation, no misgivings, no care, no anxiety. भगवान् (*bhagavān*), the Lord. एव (*eva*), alone सर्वदा (*sarvadā*), always. सर्वभावेन (*sarva-bhāvena*), with the whole heart. भजनीयः (*bhajanīyaḥ*), should be worshipped.

79. The Lord alone should be always worshipped with the whole heart by the devotees who must repose absolute trust in Him.

Cf. *Muṇḍaka Upaniṣad,* II.ii.5—

"In whom the heaven and the earth and the interval between are woven, along with the mind and all the life-breath also, know that one Self alone; give up all other talks; this is the bridge of immortality."

If this is not practicable, the aspirant should sign the name of the Lord.

सः कीर्त्यमानः शीघ्रमेवाविर्भवत्यनुभावयति भक्तान् ।। ८० ।।

सः (*saḥ*) He. कीर्त्यमानः (*kīrttyamānaḥ*), being invoked. शीघ्रम् (*śīghram*), without delay. एव (*eva*), surely. आविर्भवति (*āvirbhavati*), appears, reveals Himself. भक्तान् (*bhaktān*), the votaries. अनुभावयति (*anubhāvayati*), fills with His presence or influence.

80. Being invoked, He reveals Himself without the least delay and fills His votaries with His influences.

Cf. *Gītā,* XI.54, where Lord Kṛṣṇa says, "But, O tormentor of enemies, O Arjuna, by single-hearted devotion alone I can, in this manner, be known and beheld and penetrated to My transcendental essence. Cf. also *Bhaktiratnāvalī,* V.8.

त्रिसत्यस्य भक्तिरेव गरीयसी भक्तिरेव गरीयसी ।। ८१ ।।

भक्तिः (*bhaktiḥ*), Devotion. एव (*eva*), alone. त्रिसत्यस्य (*tri-satyasya*), that which was, that which is, and that which will be. The unchanging in lime. The eternal. गरीयसी (*garīyasī*), great.

81. Devotion alone weighs heaviest with the Eternal, devotion

alone weighs heaviest. Or, devotion to the Lord is the most glorious, devotion is the most glorious.

The meaning is this—

Even truths may change; for, "The old order changeth yielding place to new, and God fulfils Himself in many ways." But love cannot. Like God, love is eternal also.

गुणमाहात्म्यासक्तिरूपासक्तिपूजासक्तिस्मरणासक्तिदास्यासक्तिसख्यासक्तिवात्सल्यासक्ति-कान्तासक्त्यात्मनिवेदनासक्तितन्मयासक्तिपरमविरहासक्तिरूपैकधाप्येकादशधा भवति ।। ८२ ।।

एकधा (*ekadhā*), of one kind. गुणमाहात्म्यासक्तिरूपासक्तिपूजासक्तिस्मरणासक्ति-दास्यासक्तिसख्यासक्तिवात्सल्यासक्तिकान्तासक्त्यात्मनिवेदनासक्तितन्मयासक्तिपरमविरहासक्तिरूपा (*guṇamāhātmyāsakti-rūpāsakti-pūjāsakti-smaraṇāsakti-dāsyāsakti-sakhyāsakti-vātsalyāsakti-kāntāsakti-ātmanivedanāsakti-tanmayāsakti-paramavirahāsakti-rūpā*), developing in the forms of love of attributes and majesty, love of beauty, love of adoration, love of recollection, love of a servant, love of a friend, love of a parent, love of a beloved wife, love of self-dedication, love of self-absorption, and love of permanent self-effacement. एकादशधा (*ekādaśadhā*), elevenfold. भवति (*bhavati*), becomes.

82. Devotion, though one in kind, still appears in eleven forms according as it takes the course of attachment to the attributes and greatness of God, attachment to His beauty, attachment to His worship, attachment to His memories, attachment to His service, attachment to His friendship, attachment to parental affection towards Him, attachment to him (as) of a beloved wife, attachment to self-consecration, attachment to self-absorption or Godliness), and attachment to permanent self-effacement.

This *sutram* requires some explanation. The aspirant begins by singing the name of God and thereby develops the feeling of delight in the Lord. This delight in the Lord has principally two aspects. It may be excited either by the contemplation of the Lord as Power or by the contemplation of the Lord as Love. The former, i.e., attachment to God as Power, is here called by the name of, "attachment to the attributes and greatness of God", because it generally arises out of contemplation of these things. This is what the Western theologians understand by 'natural religion' which is an appreciation of God in the study of man and the world. The latter, i.e., attachment to God as Love, is here described as "attachment to His beauty", because it is principally generated by the sweetness of divine beauty. These then are the two primary coordinate stages in the evolution of supreme love. The next is the stage of worship, of quiet, selfless adoration of the Deity, which is followed by attachment to the memories of the Lord. This ceaseless contemplation of His power and performances gradually establishes some sort of personal relationship between the Lord and His Love. It is called 'personal love' and it unfolds itself into four successively higher stages. First of all the devotee serves the Lord as a servant serves his master. Then he approaches Him nearer and behave towards Him as a friend does towards a friend. The relationship is then felt to be more closely personal and the devotee rises higher and manifests parental affection for the Loved One, as a father to his son. And lastly, the little remaining remoteness between them vanishes altogether and the two become one in spirit; and the devotee develops all the marks of a beloved wife's love for her beloved husband. This last, i.e., "attachment (as) of a wife", again has two moments, according as the sense of power or the sense of Love, is dominant in it, the sense of Love being sequent to the sense of Power. The 'attachment (as) of a wife' under the sense of Love results in the complete consecration of the self to the service of the Lord; and therefore, it has been here called 'attachment to self-consecration'. This in its turn rises into the stages of self-absorption or God-vision when the devotee feels the living presence of God anywhere and everywhere and permanently loses himself in the Lord. (Vide *supra*, pp. xviii, xxii.)

In the *Kitāb-al-Luma*, the oldest treatise on Sufism, the following ten 'states' (spiritual feelings and dispositions) have been enumerated—meditation, nearness to God, love, fear, hope, longing, intimacy, tranquillity, contemplation, and certainty. "They descend", says the author, "from God into his heart, without his being able to repel them when they come, or to retain them when they go."

इत्येवं वदन्ति जनजल्पनिर्भया एकमताः कुमारव्यासशुकशाण्डिल्यगर्गविष्णु-कौण्डिल्यशेषोद्धवारुणिबलिहनुमद्विभीषणादयोभक्त्याचार्याः ।। ८३ ।।

जनजल्पनिर्भयाः (*jana-jalpa-nirbhayāḥ*), fearless of the clamour of the crowd. एकमताः (*ekamatāḥ*), of one opinion; unanimous. कुमारव्यासशुकशाण्डिल्यगर्गविष्णुकौण्डिल्यशेषोद्धवारुणिबलिहनुमद्विभीषणादयः Sanatkumāra, Vyāsa, Śuka, Śāṇḍilya, Garga, Viṣṇu Kauṇḍilya, Śeṣa, Uddhava, Āruṇi, Bali, Hanumat, Vibhīṣaṇa, and others. भक्त्याचार्याः (*bhaktyācāryāḥ*), teachers of devotion. इति (*iti*), thus. एवं (*evaṃ*), in this strain. वदन्ति (*vadanti*), say.

83. Thus, the teachers of devotion, Sanatkumāra, Vyāsa, Śuka, Sāṇḍilya, Garga, Viṣṇu, Kauṇḍilya, Śeṣa, Uddhava, Āruṇi, Bali, Hanumat, Vibhīṣaṇa, and others, declare unanimously, in this strain, being fearless of the clamour of the crowd.

यः इदं नारदप्रोक्तं शिवानुशासनं विश्वसिति श्रद्धत्ते सः भक्तिमान्भवति सः प्रेष्ठं लभते सः प्रेष्ठं लभते इति।। ८४।।

यः (*yaḥ*), who. नारदप्रोक्तं (*nārada-proktaṃ*), recited by Nārada. इदं (*idaṃ*), this. शिवानुशासनं (*śiva-anuśāsanaṃ*), wholesome teaching. विश्वसिति (*viśvasiti*), believes in. श्रद्धत्ते (*śraddhatte*), has faith in. सः (*saḥ*), he. भक्तिमान् (*bhaktimān*), possessed of devotion. भवति (*bhavati*), becomes. प्रेष्ठं (*preṣṭhaṃ*), the dearest. लभते (*labhate*) obtains. इति (*iti*), this word marks the end of the treatise.

84. He who believes and has faith in this wholesome doctrine expounded by Nārada, becomes possessed of devotion, he reaches to the dearest, reaches to the dearest.

Index of the Aphorisms

Index